Maelor Way

INCLUDING CIRCULAR WALKS USING THE LLANGOLLEN CANAL

Publication, text, maps and illustrations (except where otherwise stated) by

Gordon Emery
27 Gladstone Road, Chester

©1991

Produced on recycled paper by
MASONS THE PRINTERS

credits

Thanks to Fred Broad,
Frank Wainwright, Lorna Allen
John Marchant, Elspeth Pope
and Janet Pinder, not
forgetting local people
who showed me interesting
features on the Way.

I would also like to thank
the staff of the Clwyd
and Shropshire Records
Offices and Libraries.

ISBN 1 872265 98 7

cover

'Looking over Hanmer Mere'

by Mike Penney
Storm Photography
0244 377170

contents

Introduction   4
Origin of the Way   6
How to use this guide   8
Starting points & distances   10
Ordnance Survey maps   12
Location map   13

Walk directions and maps followed by points of interest:
section I   Grindley Brook/Wolvesacre   14
section II Wolvesacre/Kiln Green   20
section III Kiln Green/Whitewell Church   26
section IV Whitewell Church / New Hall Farm   30
section V   New Hall Farm / Llyn Bedydd   36
section VI Llyn Bedydd / Hanmer   38
section VII Hanmer / Brook Lane   42
section VIII Brook Lane/Penley   50
section IX Penley / Cross Mill   56
section X   Cross Mill / Overton   58
section XI Overton / Shell Brook   60
section XII Shell Brook / Flannog Farm   70
section XIII Flannog Farm / Glynmorlas   76
section XIV Glynmorlas / Gledrid Bridge   80
section XV Gledrid Bridge / Chirk Bank   84
section XVI Chirk Bank / Pont Faen   90
section XVII Pont Faen / Bronygarth   96

Around the mere, a circular walk from Hanmer   102
Return beside the Llangollen Canal   104
Extension to Pontcysyllte   113
Other long distance trails linking with the Maelor Way   117
Further reading   121
Complaints   122
Walking Groups in the area   123
Directory of Services for the Maelor Way   124

introduction

The Maelor Way is a 24 mile / 38 kilometre waymarked cross-country trail using public footpaths, lanes and a canal towpath.

At the eastern end it links with three waymarked routes at Grindley Brook, near Whitchurch. These are the Sandstone Trail, the South Cheshire Way, and the Shropshire Way. The western end meets Offa's Dyke Path at Bronygarth, near Chirk. Near both ends, the Way also meets the Llangollen Canal.

Most of the Maelor Way is easy walking across pleasant meadows and through woodlands. Many parts of the walk follow waterways : Grindley Brook, the Llangollen Canal, and the rivers Dee and Ceiriog. The Way also passes through three villages : Overton, with its ancient yew trees, one of the seven wonders of Wales; Penley where the Polish Hospital once boosted the population threefold ; and Hanmer, situated on the mere which gave the village and its local aristocracy their name.

Parts of the route are muddy in winter.

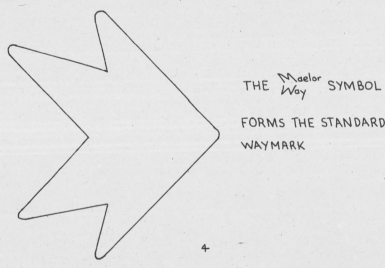

THE Maelor Way SYMBOL

FORMS THE STANDARD WAYMARK

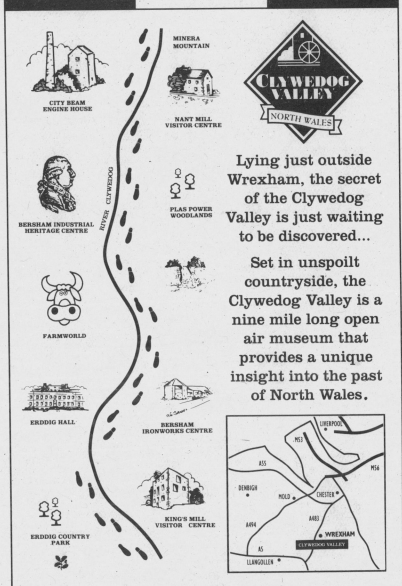

CITY BEAM ENGINE HOUSE

MINERA MOUNTAIN

NANT MILL VISITOR CENTRE

CLYWEDOG VALLEY NORTH WALES

BERSHAM INDUSTRIAL HERITAGE CENTRE

RIVER CLYWEDOG

PLAS POWER WOODLANDS

FARMWORLD

ERDDIG HALL

BERSHAM IRONWORKS CENTRE

ERDDIG COUNTRY PARK

KING'S MILL VISITOR CENTRE

Lying just outside Wrexham, the secret of the Clywedog Valley is just waiting to be discovered...

Set in unspoilt countryside, the Clywedog Valley is a nine mile long open air museum that provides a unique insight into the past of North Wales.

LIVERPOOL
M53
A55
M56
DENBIGH
MOLD
CHESTER
A483
A494
WREXHAM
CLYWEDOG VALLEY
A5
LLANGOLLEN

For further information:
Tourism Development Officer, Guildhall, Wrexham,
Clwyd LL11 1AY. Telephone: (0978) 290444

origin of the way

The route for the Maelor Link (as it was originally known) was planned by Jack Baker (1910-81) to join the Sandstone Trail, for which he was largely responsible, with Offa's Dyke Path, which he had also worked on.

Jack Baker was a regular contributor to the Liverpool Echo where, under the pen-name 'Rambler' he published walks complete with bus times and fares from Liverpool:

> 'Train or bus to Flint — train fare is 8/3d return, Crosville L8 bus is cheaper (6/2d return) and there are buses from Woodside at 9.20, 10.20, 12.20 and 14.20 (50) on weekdays'

Collections of these walks were later published in paperback by the Echo. These were '20 Walks in Mid-Cheshire', '20 Walks in Wirral', '20 Walks in South West Lancashire' and '20 Walks in North Wales'.

Jack's many books and articles on walking include 'Walks in Clwyd' which I have now republished in greater detail with illustrations and notes.

Jack Baker also founded the Mid-Cheshire Footpath Society, a still-flourishing, walking and campaigning group. Jack's knowledge of footpaths must have been extensive: while sorting through his files I came across a circular walk on a map of Clwyd — it was numbered 227. A memorial to him is situated on the Sandstone Trail, two kilometres south of Frodsham, at grid reference SJ 515763.

When Jack died, work on the Maelor Link ceased until Justin McCarthy the Footpath Secretary of the Mid-Cheshire Footpath Society met a Wrexham Maelor Council officer, Ian Anderson, on a train.

Wrexham Maelor Borough Council took on the project and included the route on the local plan. They conducted an initial survey which showed over 40 obstructions on the route but, due to lack of finances, the plan was shelved. After some time it was suggested that the Manpower Services Commission take on the work under their Community Programme but when the scheme finished, plans for the path were still in their infancy, although Ian had designed a logo to go with the trail's new name: the Maelor Way.

In 1989 I became the Ramblers' Association Footpath Inspector for the Wrexham area and offered to work on the Way in return for travelling expenses. The Countryside Commission and the Borough Council shared the cost.

Clwyd County Council supplied stile kits and bridges in Clwyd while Shropshire County Council did the s me across the border. Cheshire and Shropshire county councils signposted both ends of the trail.

Together with an out-of-work landscape gardener, Bob Symmons, I resurveyed the route, cleared the paths and erected signposts, stiles and waymarkers. Paths in Hanmer were so bad that we erected a further 20 stiles on nearby paths and a route around the mere.

Unfortunately Bob had omitted to inform the Employment Office, with the result that we were secretly followed by government officials until it was explained that he was working voluntarily.

Despite other minor difficulties, the Maelor Way was opened on April 6th 1991 by the Mayor of Wrexham Maelor, Councillor Malcolm Williams.

how to use this guide

Unlike almost all other linear trail guides which only give route directions one way, this guide also caters for the 50% of walkers who might like to walk the other way.

Each page of directions is split into Westwards and Eastwards (although in reality certain sections of the Way occasionally run from north to south). However the walker from the west (ie Bronygarth) will have to read the walk directions starting from section XVII and working forwards.

No further maps are needed for the route although Ordnance Survey maps covering the area are listed on page 12.

Short extensions to interesting places are given *in italics*. Numbers in brackets [] refer to points of interest.

At the back of the book are directions for a circular route using the Llangollen Canal towpath in conjuction with the Maelor Way. There are also short summaries of other trails that link to the Way.

Finally there is a directory of services to help you plan your walk, rest and refreshment. Accommodation near the Maelor Way is limited, so book well in advance.

Please remember, shut all gates, leave no litter and do not disturb wildlife. Walkers with dogs are legally bound to keep them under close control on rights-of-way where there is farmstock; in most cases you are advised to keep your dog on a lead especially in lambing season.

All paths used are public (except for two short permissive paths courtesy of two helpful farmers). Please keep to the waymarked route.

starting points and distances

MAELOR WAY   24 miles / 38 kilometres

Start at either:

Grindley Brook, near Whitchurch, at the junction of the Chester-Whitchurch road (A41) and the Malpas road (B5395).
Grid reference SJ 522432

Trains to Whitchurch (Crewe-Shrewsbury line)
Buses to Grindley Brook (Whitchurch-Malpas-Chester route)

or:

Castle Mill Bridge, Bronygarth near Chirk (below the B4500).
Grid reference SJ 263375

Trains to Chirk (Chester-Shrewsbury line)
Buses to Chirk (Wrexham-Oswestry route)
            (Llangollen-Chirk route occasional)

Parking space is limited at both ends. Why not leave your car, and your cares, at home? From Shrewsbury or Chester you can reach both ends of the route by public transport.

- - - - - - - - - - - - - - - - - - -

MAELOR WAY CIRCULAR WALK returning beside the canal
            47 miles / 76 kilometres
Start at either Grindley Brook or Bronygarth

- - - - - - - - - - - - - - - - - - -

MAELOR WAY EXTENDED CIRCULAR WALK including Offa's Dyke Path to Pontcysyllte Aqueduct and returning beside the Llangollen Canal
            56 miles / 90 kilometres

Start at either Grindley Brook or Bronygarth

SHORTER CIRCULAR WALK 1 The Maelor Way from Grindley Brook to Penley, Lanes to Ellesmere (see Location Map) and return beside the Llangollen Canal.

28 miles / 45 kilometres

Start at Grindley Brook.

— — — — — — — — — — — — — — —

SHORTER CIRCULAR WALK 2 The Maelor Way from Bronygarth to Penley, Lanes to Ellesmere (see Location Map) and return beside the canal.

24 miles / 39 kilometres

— — — — — — — — — — — — — — —

Shorter circular walks can be made by either: heading south on any road from the Maelor Way between Grindley Brook and Chirk to return beside the canal

or: returning on nearby lanes shown on the section maps.

— — — — — — — — — — — — — — —

A longer walk can be made by using the Shropshire Way from Grindley Brook to Clun. From here head north on the Offa's Dyke Path to Bronygarth.

— — — — — — — — — — — — — — —

GRID REFERENCES for the other 16 points given in the section maps are:

Wolvesacre SJ 508432   Kil(n) Green SJ 496430

Whitewell Church SJ495414   New Hall Farm SJ 490397

Llyn Bedydd SJ 471393   Hanmer SJ 455396

Brook Lane SJ 418397   Penley SJ 419397

Cross Mill SJ 404411   Overton SJ 373419

Shell Brook SJ 350412 (No vehicular access)

Flannog Farm SJ 326401   Glynmorlas SJ 313377

Gledrid Bridge SJ 298368   Chirk Bank SJ 291370

Pont Faen SJ 280370

Car users should ensure that access to fields is not obstructed and remember that wide agricultural machinery has to use narrow lanes. Always ask permission at public house car parks.

ordnance survey maps

These maps are not necessary to walk the Maelor Way but are listed for reference and so that circular walks can be planned.

Please note that, although Wrexham Maelor Borough Council have embarked upon a programme of revitalising their public rights-of-way network, not all paths in the area are yet signposted or even clear of obstructions.

1:50 000 LANDRANGER SERIES

117 Chester, Wrexham & surrounding area
126 Shrewsbury & surrounding area

1:25 000 PATHFINDER SERIES

806 Llangollen and Wrexham (Wrecsam) South   SJ 24/34
807 Whitchurch (Shropshire) and Malpas (Cheshire) SJ 44/54
827 Chirk (Y Waun)   SJ 23/33
828 Ellesmere (East) and Prees   SJ 43/53

DEFINITIVE MAPS OF PUBLIC RIGHTS OF WAY

These Ordnance Survey maps overlaid with numbered footpaths, bridleways and byways open to all traffic were produced under The National Parks and Access to the Countryside Act 1949 and The Countryside Act 1968 (as amended). They are not for sale but can be studied at the following:

WREXHAM MAELOR BOROUGH   Rhostyllen House, Rhostyllen, Wrexham.

CLWYD COUNTY COUNCIL (including Wrexham) Shire Hall, Mold.

SHROPSHIRE COUNTY COUNCIL   Winston Churchill Building, Radbrook Centre, Shrewsbury; District Council Offices; Whitchurch Library.

CHESHIRE COUNTY COUNCIL   County Hall, Chester; Reference Library, Chester.

TITHE MAPS

The 1835/45 maps recording owners, occupiers and tithes can be studied at the respective County Records Office for the area. Clwyd records are still split into Denbighshire (Ruthin CRO) and Flintshire (Hawarden CRO). Proof of identity and, in some cases, an appointment is needed.

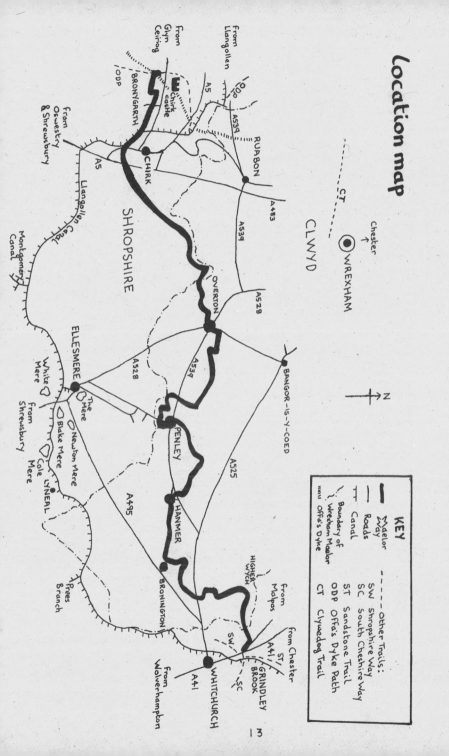

Location map

KEY

▬▬▬	Maelor Way
────	Roads
━┿━	Canal
— — —	Boundary of Wrexham Maelor
⋯⋯⋯	Offa's Dyke

Other Trails:
- SW   Shropshire Way
- SC   South Cheshire Way
- ST   Sandstone Trail
- ODP Offa's Dyke Path
- CT   Clywedog Trail

CLWYD

SHROPSHIRE

from Glyn Ceiriog

from Llangollen

ODP

BRONYGARTH

Chirk castle

RUABON

A5

A539

A539

A483

CHIRK

from Oswestry & Shrewsbury

A5

Llangollen Canal

Montgomery Canal

CT

chester →

WREXHAM

N

OVERTON

A528

A539

A528

BANGOR-IS-Y-COED

ELLESMERE

White Mere

The Mere

Blake Mere

Cole Mere

Newton Mere

LYNEAL

from Shrewsbury

A495

A525

PENLEY

HANMER

BRONINGTON

Prees Branch

HIGHER WYCH

from Malpas

from Chester

ST / A41

GRINDLEY BROOK

SW

SC

WHITCHURCH

from Wolverhampton

A41

westwards GRINDLEY BROOK to WOLVESACRE

Follow the Malpas road [1] from the A41 junction. Cross the small stone bridge over Grindley Brook [2]. Fifty metres farther on, beyond the red-brick house 'Edgefield', is the first stile on the Maelor Way. Go ahead through the fields [3] over wooden stiles, but do not take any of the stiles or the gate leading across the brook to your left.

Cross the concrete bridge at the end of the fifth field. Beyond the gate ahead, the path follows a disused mill-leat and then descends through a gate beside the red-brick stable of Wolvesacre Mill [4].

On leaving the driveway turn left up the lane.

eastwards WOLVESACRE to GRINDLEY BROOK

At the foot of the hill turn right along the driveway to Wolvesacre Mill [4]. Continue past the stables into the field. The path now follows the disused mill-leat on your right. Ignore a gateway over the leat but take the gate ahead and veer slightly left to cross a concrete bridge. Keep to the right-hand boundary in the next five fields [3]. Ignore stiles and a gate leading across the brook.

RED
CAMPION
Silene dioica

A house stands to the right as you approach the last stile on the Maelor Way. Turn right onto the Malpas road [1] and cross a small stone bridge over Grindley Brook [2] to reach the A41 junction. Across the road a lane leads to the Llangollen Canal and other long-distance trails. (See later chapters for details.)

NOT TO SCALE

Some areas have been expanded

to show directions in detail.

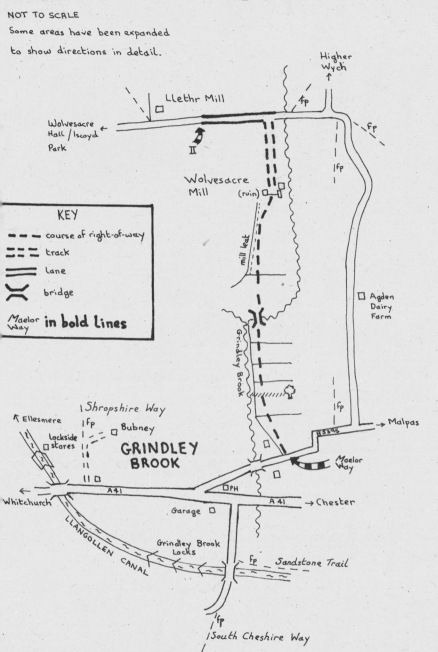

Llethr Mill

Wolvesacre
Hall / Iscoyd
Park

Higher
Wych

Wolvesacre
Mill
(ruin)

mill leat

Grindley Brook

Agden
Dairy
Farm

KEY

- - - - course of right-of-way

⫶⫶⫶⫶ track

‗‗‗‗ lane

⟩⟨ bridge

Maelor Way in bold lines

Shropshire Way

↖ Ellesmere

Lockside
stores

Bubney

**GRINDLEY
BROOK**

Malpas

Maelor
Way

B5395

PH

A41

Garage

← Whitchurch

A 41 → Chester

LLANGOLLEN CANAL

Grindley Brook
Locks

fp Sandstone Trail

fp

South Cheshire Way

points of interest

[1] Much of this road lies almost parallel to the Roman military road from Chester via Whitchurch to Wroxeter. Distances in Roman miles (approximately a kilometre - a thousand paces) between the forts were given in the Itinery of Antonius as follows:

DEVA IX BOVIVM XX MEDIOLANO XII RUTINIO XI URICONIO
(Chester 9 Holt 20 Whitchurch 12 Bury Walls 11 Wroxeter)

[2] John Ogilby's map of 1675 depicting the Chester to Bristol road shows the brook and 'Grinsley bridg'.

The name probably derives from 'grin' (green) and 'ley' (open tract of land).

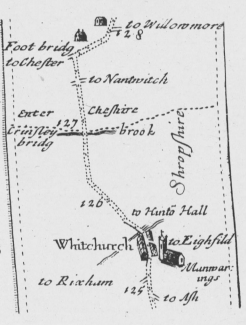

PART OF
JOHN OGILBY'S
ROAD MAP

[3] In one field a central ridge and a lone oak mark the probable course of the Roman road mentioned earlier, a straight course to a small hilltop west of Whitchurch. It also shows the hedge scarp: a former boundary where earth built up on the eastern side due to ploughing over the years. In another, the Way crosses a rabbit warren dug into the sandy soil.

Unlike our native hare, the common rabbit *Oryctolagus cuniculus* originally came from Spain or North Africa. Introduced to this country by the Normans and named the coney (only the young were called rabbits or rabbets), it was first bred in coney warrens. Conery Lane in Bronington, near the Maelor Way is an example of a place name relating to this animal, as is The Warren in Iscoyd.

The warrener would regularly cull rabbits for their meat and fur. In 1690 it was estimated that 2 million rabbits were bred as opposed to 3.2 million sheep and 1·3 million pigs. Whether this figure extended to Wales is hard to ascertain for in 1796 Pennant recorded 31 mammals in Holywell and Whitford but omitted the rabbit.

With the decline of the feudal system, rabbits that had gone wild spread over the countryside causing crop damage, soil erosion, and injury to young trees. With the advances in land reclamation, land that had formerly been moorland was drained and enclosed, while land that had been sandy was rejuvenated by the use of marl [see 17], so that crops of wheat or hay could be grown. Rabbits became to be seen as a pest. As a result, in 1880 the Ground Game Act 1880 allowed tenants to catch animals on land that they farmed. (Originally common law allowed this but estate owners through the centuries had put restrictions on tenants to keep the game from the 'lower classes'.) As tenant farmers added to their income most of the large warrens (200 hectares or so) became unprofitable and were broken up.

By 1930 the British rabbit population had reached 50 million and although, in some parts of the country, wire fencing and extermination techniques were becoming effective (the Forestry Commission spent £500,000 on fencing) by 1950 there may have been 100 million rabbits in Britain even though rabbits were hunted whenever there was an 'r' in the month.

The scourge of Myxomatosis in 1953 nearly wiped out the population, killing 99% of the breed. I was born that year and never saw a healthy rabbit until after 10 years of age.

I

The deadly Myxomatosis virus, endemic in the South American rabbit and transmitted by fleas, had first been deliberately introduced to Australia, and then to France in 1952. It spread to Britain and in turn was spread rapidly by farmers who would travel to affected areas and bring back diseased rabbits. Needless to say, growths on the rabbit discouraged their use as food especially as some eating the diseased animal claimed to have caught a fever as a direct result.

The enormous fertility rate of rabbits is partly controlled by its predators: fox, eagle, buzzard, polecat, stoat, weasel, rat, snake and man, although cold winters are the biggest killer for this Mediterranean animal. Meanwhile if a warren is overcrowded some of the males will be evicted by the head buck and if there is a local food shortage the does can dissolve the embryos in their own bodies and suppress oestroegen production.

The territory of a rabbit warren is marked out by secretions from anal and inguinal glands in the animal, and the head buck also smears the other animals in the community by the same method. The centre of the warren is the abode of the head buck who protects the head doe by fighting off and urinating on the other bucks. Does do all the excavation work. The warren itself is protected by an alarm system whereby the rabbits on the outer edges drum their hind feet on the ground to warn of intruders.

Although mating occurs all the year round, with even sterile rabbits indulging, the female only gives birth between spring and the end of summer when up to six litters may be produced, all at night. These are walled off in underground tunnels so that predators cannot eat them. The mother only visits them once

18

each night, for a short period, to feed them.

Rabbits are vegetarians and eat almost any vegetable matter except cowslip, comfrey, rhododendron, burdock and sorrel. Even the bark of trees is consumed in harsh winters. Unlike domestic rabbits they do not drink water, receiving all their liquid nourishment from vegetation. They pass food through their stomach twice, by eating their soft night droppings to obtain the vitamin B12 and beneficial bacteria which are formed in the lower intestine, too late for them to absorb the first time.

Interestingly the bible forbade the use of rabbits as a food in Leviticus, chapter 11 which states 'Nevertheless ye shall not eat of them that cheweth the cud and — the coney, because he cheweth the cud but divideth not the hoof; he is unclean to you'.

Of the three main varieties of rabbit introduced to Britain the common-grey is the most common while occasionally the silver-grey can be seen. Black rabbits were introduced to offshore islands although I have seen one in Chirk and another near Prestatyn. Will the population of our long-eared furry friends grow to their pre-Myxomatosis level or will their growth rate be controlled? One thing is certain — they breed like rabbits.

[4] Wolvesacre Mill can be seen opposite the cottage. It bears an inscribed date of 1801. Formerly there were two cottages here, one for the miller and one for his worker.

The area is said to be where the last Welsh wolf was shot and a stone in a small 'craft' (field) downstream (on private property) is said to mark the spot. However, an alternative theory is that the name was derived from Hwva's acre. Hwva was the steward to Owain Gwynedd, the 12th century prince of Wales.

westwards WOLVESACRE to KILN GREEN

Less than a kilometre ahead is Wolvesacre Hall [5] and 500 metres beyond that, Iscoyd Park [6]. However, the Maelor Way continues over the stile on your right immediately past Llethr Mill (hillside mill). Head for a gateway in the centre of the far boundary. On your right is a row of mature oaks [7].

Continue to the next field boundary and go through the bridlegate (a small gate). Take the stile directly ahead and then, keeping the protruding field corner on your left, follow the raised track to the lane. The farm is Maes y Groes [8]. Look to your right to see the black and white building of Bank Farm [9] across the valley in Higher Wych [10]. On your left is Henrwst Smithy.

Turn right, then immediately left along the lane signposted to 'KILN GREEN' [11].

eastwards KILN GREEN to WOLVESACRE

Across the valley is the black and white Bank Farm [9] in Higher Wych [10]. At the T-junction signposted 'KILN GREEN' [11] turn right. Ahead is Henrwst Smithy.

Take the stile on your left opposite the farm, Maes y Groes [8]. Follow the raised track to the field corner then continue ahead over a stile, past an oak tree, and through a bridlegate. Now veer slightly left to go through the gateway on the far boundary and then continue in the same direction to the far corner of the field, near a red brick building, Llethr Mill (hillside mill). On your left is a line of oaks [7] and on your right, Wolvesacre Hall [5]. At the lane turn left unless you wish to see the Hall, a kilometre up the track, or Iscoyd Park [6], 500 metres farther still.

HENRWST SMITHY (Private) 17th Century.

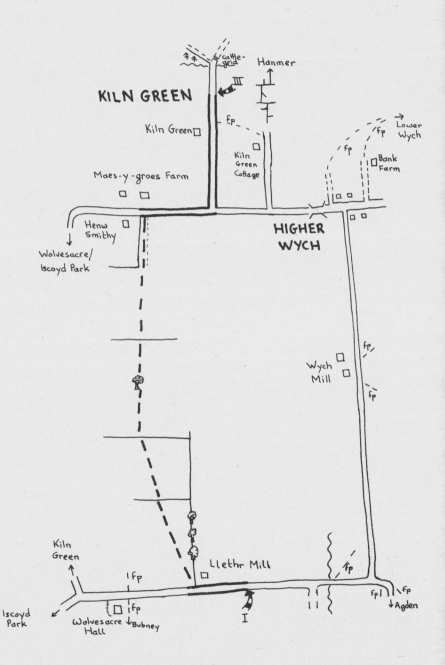

KILN GREEN

Kiln Green

Maes-y-groes Farm

Henw Smithy

Wolvesacre/ Iscoyd Park

cattle-grid

III

Hanmer

fp

Kiln Green Cottage

fp

fp

Lower Wych

fp

Bank Farm

HIGHER WYCH

Wych Mill

fp

fp

Kiln Green

fp

Iscoyd Park

fp

Wolvesacre Hall

Bubney

Llethr Mill

I

fp

fp

fp

Agden

points of interest

[5] Wolvesacre Hall (private) lies on the moated site of an earlier structure. The southern part of the three remaining sides of the moat is visible from the track.

[6] 'Iscoed' (below the wood) was sold to Sir Thomas Hanmer, Mr Lloyd of Halghton and Mr John Bridgeson for 1000 guineas in 1656. The present brick house was built for Sir William Hanmer in the early 18th century and altered for P.L. Godsal who bought the property in the 1840's. There were also small additions made for his son in the late 19th century. The outbuildings include a square dovecote. Iscoyd Hall is private property but some views are obtainable from the public road.

In 1737 Edward Hughes, an ordained Roman Catholic priest, was arrested here for giving mass; many of the local families had a history of recusancy (not going to Church of England services).

In 1885 a bronze axe head was found in the grounds.

During 1938, the German foreign minister, von Ribbentrop, stayed at Iscoyd Park and visited the Chester races. Only eight years later he was hanged for war crimes.

[7] These oaks form much of the remaining field boundary. Unfortunately many of the standard trees in hedgerows, each one an important wildlife habitat, are now becoming old and being removed without suitable replacements being planted. Modern hedge flailing methods only add to the problem.

Oak trees in particular are one of the most valuable hedgerow standards, not just because of their wildlife value, supporting an enormous quantity and variety of insects — in turn a food for birds — but as a source of native hardwood timber.

Galls on oak trees are caused by the infestation of parasitic
insects and have been used for both ink making and Christmas
decorations. The examples below are from mid-19th century engravings.

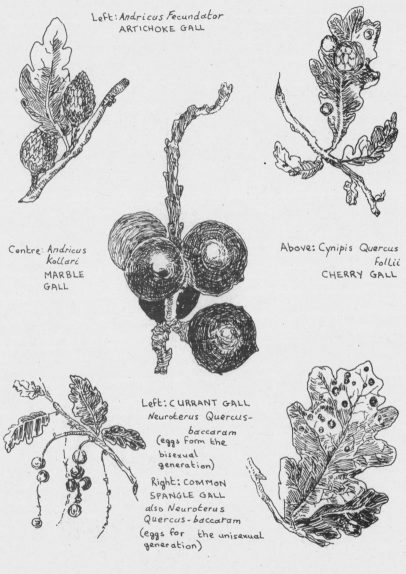

Left: *Andricus Fecundator*
ARTICHOKE GALL

Centre: *Andricus Kollari*
MARBLE GALL

Above: *Cynipis Quercus Follii*
CHERRY GALL

Left: CURRANT GALL
Neuroterus Quercus-baccaram
(eggs form the bisexual generation)

Right: COMMON SPANGLE GALL
also *Neuroterus Quercus-baccaram*
(eggs for the unisexual generation)

OAK GALLS OF CYNIPIDS (GALL WASPS)

[8] Maes y Groes (field of the cross) is said to have had a shrine in it at one time and, interestingly enough, the old farm buildings shown on the Ordnance Survey map also form a rough cross. In 1879 three carved stones, said to be Saxon or Norman, were found in the floor of a cow-shed and taken to Iscoyd Hall to decorate the patio. An engraving of these can be found in 'Ancient and Historical Monuments' for the County of Flint'.

[9] Bank Farm is a listed building dating from the Elizabethan period. The front once had a timber frame but much of this has been replaced with brick. The upper halves of the two wall posts and the tie beam remain but the rest is merely black paint. Footpaths lead past this private residence.

BANK FARM

[10] This area has been proposed as the missing manor of 'Burwadestone' mentioned in the Domesday Book of William the Conqueror.

'From Earl Hugo (Hugh of Chester), Robert son of Hugo holds Burwadestone. Earl Edwin held it (before 1066). 5 hides paying geld (tax). Tillage for 14 ploughs (about 560 hectares). In Lordship 1. 12 villagers and 2 smallholders with 3 ploughs. 1 man-at-arms has 1 plough, another man-at-arms holds ½ hide which pays him 12s (60p). A salthouse at 24s. Value before (1066) £6.4s; now 54s; found waste. This manor was 2 leagues long and 1 wide. The Bishop of Chester claims 1½ hides and a salthouse from this manor.'

Compared to other manors this seems quite well off, with a

population of about 70 people. No wonder the Bishop was putting in a claim.

The name wych, wich or wic is Saxon for salt-town and it is probable that salt has been mined in Cheshire since Roman times or before. By the Middle Ages the trade was flourishing with exports all over Britain. The Domesday Book records the special taxes and tolls and even local Laws that applied to the salt-towns Middewich, Northwich and Nantwich.

Apart from the lost manor, the earliest recorded name of Wych is Fulewic in 1096-1101. Other names are Foulwiche and Durtwich.

In the Civil War a Parliamentarian's diary records that, on 28th August 1643, 'Captain Croxton and Captain Venables, with their companions and others, went to Durtwich, and cut in pieces all their pans, pumps, salt-pits, and works and carried some of their pans off; so their salt-making was spoiled, which served Shrewsbury*and many other places in the kingdom'. This attack, no doubt put an end to the salt industry here for a while, however by 1831 there is a record of the 'Upper and Lower Wych Salt Works'.

At the foot of the hill a right turn brings you to the ruined mill, probably built on a mill-site dating from the 14th century.

The Wych Valley was surveyed for a proposed branch to the Eastern Canal of the Ellesmere Canal Company. The plans were submitted to Flintshire County Council in 1792.

[11] Kiln Green was originally Cil or Kil Green, although a survey for another branch of the Ellesmere Canal shows it as Cill Green. The name is of Welsh origin and refers to a religious retreat.

*see the circular walk around the mere for the old salt road.

westwards KILN GREEN to WHITEWELL CHURCH

Follow the lane. It descends into a valley and crosses Iscoyd Brook. Turn half left through the bridlegate, before the cattle-grid, and head up to the far corner of the field to go through another. The Way now follows the woodland boundary [12] through two fields. There are no recorded public paths in the wood.

Beyond the wood take a bridlegate on your left, then turn right up the bank to a field-gate. Follow the track ahead to go between houses. At the lane turn right and in 200 metres, opposite a driveway, turn left and cross the field. The Church of St Mary [14] at Whitewell lies ahead. Before the churchyard gate turn right and go through the kissing-gate beside the cottage. Keep the unusual thatched building [13] on your right.

eastwards WHITEWELL CHURCH to KILN GREEN

After visiting the Church of St Mary [14] continue between the unusual thatched building [13] and the cottage. Beyond the kissing-gate turn right and then, by the churchyard gate, turn left to cross the field. At the lane turn right and after 200 metres take the track between houses on your left.

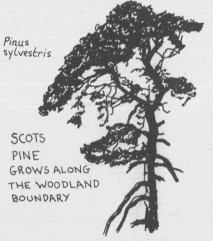

Pinus sylvestris

SCOTS PINE GROWS ALONG THE WOODLAND BOUNDARY

Ignore a track to your left after 300 metres but continue ahead into a field. After a few metres, drop down to a bridlegate on your left. Turn right outside the woodland boundary [12] through three fields. At the lane turn right, soon passing Kiln Green Farm on your right.

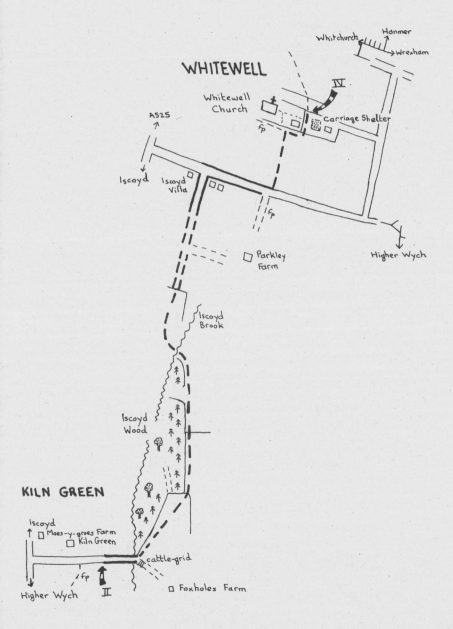

WHITEWELL

KILN GREEN

points of interest

[12] Had history taken a different course you would have been walking along a towpath now, for the surveyor's plan of 1793 shows the proposed Eastern Canal of the Ellesmere Canal Company along the top of these woods going north towards Tattenhall and the Chester Canal, and south towards Ellesmere.

The bluebell is probably our most-loved woodland plant. In the Middle Ages a gum was produced from its sap to fix feathers on the shafts of arrows.

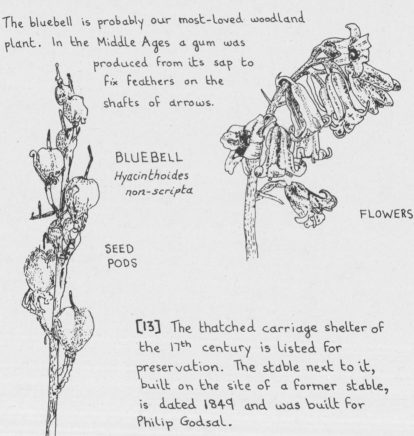

BLUEBELL
Hyacinthoides non-scripta

SEED PODS

FLOWERS

[13] The thatched carriage shelter of the 17th century is listed for preservation. The stable next to it, built on the site of a former stable, is dated 1849 and was built for Philip Godsal.

[14] St Mary's Church was built in 1830 on the site of a timber-framed chapel-of-ease formerly in the parish of Malpas, Cheshire, although it only became a 'church'

in 1885. Drawings of the old chapel can be found in the small vestry through the door at the far end of the church. Records of the chapel date from 1570 but it is believed that the site dates from Saxon times.

WHITEWELL CHURCH AND CARRIAGE SHELTER

On the 20th May 1657 the following was recorded: 'The said jurors upon their oathes doe find that the Chapell of Whitewell, in the township of Iscoide, is in the County of fflint and that the Tithes of the Township of Iscoide are annexed and belong to ye p'sh Church of Malpas, wh is in ye County of Chester.' The jurors asked that the chapel be annexed to Iscoyd but it remained part of Malpas until about 1840.

The visitor will notice that the stained-glass window is dedicated to the memory of Philip Lake Godsal of nearby Iscoyd Park, who died in 1858 aged 73. It is more difficult to see the 64 cm diameter bell, inscribed in 1898 with the names of the two church-wardens, two sidesmen and the rector.

westwards WHITEWELL CHURCH to NEW HALL FARM

Take the gate opposite the cottage and continue past the well, one of three near the church. Cross two fields to a kissing-gate at the lane. Turn left and fork right at the junction. Spring walkers will notice a red horsechestnut tree [15] in a field beside the lane. Cross the main road [16] and go through the gate ahead.

Go slightly right across two fields to the lane. Take the stile opposite and remain by the left-hand boundary to cross a bridge. After a bridge on your left continue in the same direction as before, now with the boundary on your right. Beyond a third bridge, turn left and follow the hedge halfway round the field, ignoring two gateways to use a stile by the third. Follow the right-hand boundary. The path goes beside the pond [17] towards the farm [18].

eastwards NEW HALL FARM to WHITEWELL CHURCH

The path opposite the farm [18] goes beside the pond [17]. Beyond two more stiles go anti-clockwise halfway around the large field, ignoring gateways, to cross a footbridge. On a hot day this is a good place to rest as the breeze is funnelled onto the bridge by a 'V' formation of hedges.

Keep to the left-hand boundary until you reach another bridge. Beyond this, continue in the same direction to cross another and then proceed ahead to the lane. Take the stile opposite and veer slightly left through two fields towards the main road [16]. Take the Whitewell road opposite. Spring walkers will notice a red horsechestnut tree [15] in a nearby field.

Fork left at the junction. In about 200 metres go through the kissing-gate on your right and follow the path across two fields. You soon arrive at Whitewell Church.

BRONINGTON

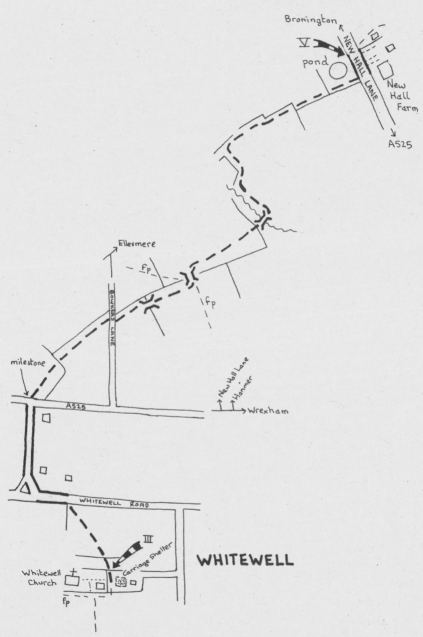

Bronington

V

NEW HALL LANE

pond

New Hall Farm

A525

Ellesmere

fp

fp

BOWKERS LANE

milestone

A525

New Hall Lane

Hanmer

Wrexham

WHITEWELL ROAD

III

Carriage Shelter

WHITEWELL

Whitewell Church

Fp

points of interest

[15] The red horsechestnut *aesculus × carnea* is a hybrid between common horsechestnut, a native of Asia and Eastern Europe, and red buckeye, a North American species. However, unlike most hybrids, it can be cultivated from seed although 'grafts' have brighter flowers.

Fruit of the tree is smaller and less spikey than that of our common horsechestnut.

Another red horsechestnut can be seen from the Maelor Way when you pass Mere House in Hanmer.

[16] This road, now the A525, was used by Daniel Defoe on his journey around Britain early in the 1720's. Later it became known as the Bangor Turnpike, the former toll road between Wrexham and Whitchurch. Meetings of the turnpike trustees were held in the Buck Inn, Bangor from 1805 and later at the Buck, Willington (see section map VIII), in the Lion, Hanmer (now the Village Arms) and in the Red Lion at Ellesmere.

The almost illegible milestone beside the footpath signpost gives the distance to Wrexham as XIII miles and the distance to Whitchurch as III. Problems of vandalism to milestones were dealt with by an Act of Parliament (see the notice reproduced opposite).

[17] Most of the lowland fields of Clwyd, Cheshire and Shropshire have a pond in them. Originally, many of these were dug for 'marl'. The marl (clay containing minerals), present at lower levels of the soil structure, was spread on the fields, both to bind the topsoil and to act as a natural fertiliser. The marl pits then became animal watering holes and ponds.

Nowadays there is an awareness of the wildlife value of such ponds as they can support a variety of aquatic plants,

INJURING
MILESTONES.

WHEREAS by an Act of Parliament (3d. Geo. 4th. Chapt. 126.) It is enacted that if any Person shall wilfully break, pull up, or damage any Milestone, and be thereof convicted before a Justice of the Peace, such Person so offending, shall forfeit and pay for every such offence, any sum not exceeding

Ten Pounds.

And whereas several of the Milestones on the Turnpike Roads leading from Marchwiel to Whitchurch, and from Redbrook to Welshampton, and from Bangor to Malpas, have of late been broken or otherwise damaged:

IS HEREBY GIVEN,

That all Persons who shall be found so offending in future, will be proceeded against according to law.

BROOKES & LEE,
Clerks to the Trustees of the said Roads.

J. WALFORD. PRINTER, WHITCHURCH.

TURNPIKE NOTICE

insects and amphibia. Grants are available from the government's countryside agencies to conserve ponds for wildlife.

The reedmace (sometimes known as bulrush, although it is not a member of the rush family) forms a mass on the central island of this pond and creates a nesting habitat for mallard, coot and moorhen. The tall stems of reedmace are often seen as dried flower decorations, but beware: the mature flowerheads burst into a multitude of cotton-like seeds sticking to furniture and clothing.

> I walked past the reedmace today,
> A fluff of cotton
> On a round pond.

Poem based on 17 syllable Japanese 'haiku' form.

COOTS

[18] Note at least three ages of building at New Hall Farm, the earliest of 16th century half-timbered construction. Until this century the farm was the property of the Hanmer Estate.

NEW HALL FARM, A GRADE III LISTED BUILDING

The present owner tells the following stories which were related to him by his father:

A travelling man and bear used to use the footpaths from Hanmer on their way to Wrexham, where they would entertain in the streets. For entertainment some of the locals would spread treacle on top of the stiles on the way. The bear would not cross until he had licked them clean.

At lodgings on the journey the bear was kept in a barn. Deciding to play a practical joke, the local farmer pretended to one of his friends that he had a calf for sale. His friend was told to go into the dark barn to get the calf out. When a light was brought, the erstwhile buyer found himself face to face with a muzzled bear!

westwards NEW HALL FARM to LLYN BEDYDD

Follow the signed Way, keeping the farm to your right. Go ahead through five fields. At the lane turn left. Ignore a lane on your right but in 200 metres take the stile on your right. Cross the large field to the lane. *The village of Bronington is to your left.* Take the field gate opposite, veering left to a gateway on the far boundary. Continue straight across two more fields. After the stile bear right. At the lane immediately turn right through gates and veer slightly left, ignoring stiles. Pass between a protruding field corner and a pond. Continue ahead and when the field opens out follow the central ditch to the far side. In the next field go along the left-hand boundary to the lane.

MAESLLWYN HOUSE

(Private)

A 17th century half-timbered house now listed for preservation. Restored by the owner.

eastwards LLYN BEDYDD to NEW HALL FARM

From the stile, follow the right-hand boundary.   In the next field follow the ditch. Keeping the wood on your right go ahead to a stile, on your left by a small pond, but do not cross it. Instead go straight ahead to the brick building. Beyond the gates turn left and cross three stiles in quick succession. Head across the next two fields. Veer slightly left in the third to reach the lane. *The village of Bronington is to your right.* Cross the large field ahead and turn left at the lane. At the junction go ahead and almost immediately take the gate on your right. Go straight through four fields to reach New Hall Farm. The Way uses another field and keeps the buildings to your left.

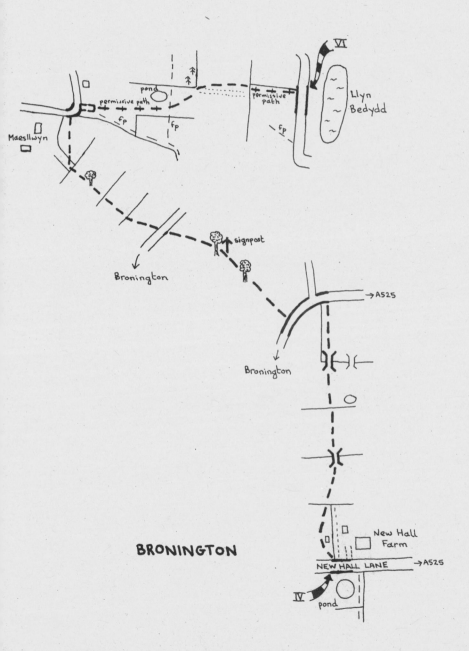

Maesllwyn

pond

permissive path

permissive path

fp

fp

fp

Llyn Bedydd

VI

signpost

Bronington

Bronington

→A525

Bronington

BRONINGTON

New Hall Farm

NEW HALL LANE

→A525

IV

pond

westwards LLYN BEDYDD to HANMER

Opposite the stile is Llyn Bedydd, a small private mere [19] almost completely hidden in woodland. Turn right and go around the corner to take the stile on your left.

Veer half-right to find a bridge and then follow the right-hand boundary of the next field to a gate at the lane.

Go through the gate opposite and turn left to a stile. Turn half-right to the stile at the top of the field and continue ahead over three more stiles. Hanmer Church Tower lies ahead. Turn right at the lane [20].

eastwards HANMER to LLYN BEDYDD

Follow the lane [20] for 150 metres or so until you reach a path leading up to your left. Cross the stile and continue in the same direction across three more, then turn half-left to another in the left-hand boundary of the field. Continue to a gate on the lane.

Go straight through the gate opposite and follow the left-hand field boundary to cross a bridge over the brook. Now veer half-right to a stile in the far corner.

Turn right along the lane and in 700 metres, ignoring one stile, cross a stile opposite Llyn Bedydd, a small private mere [19] almost completely hidden in woodland.

Veronica persica
COMMON FIELD-SPEEDWELL

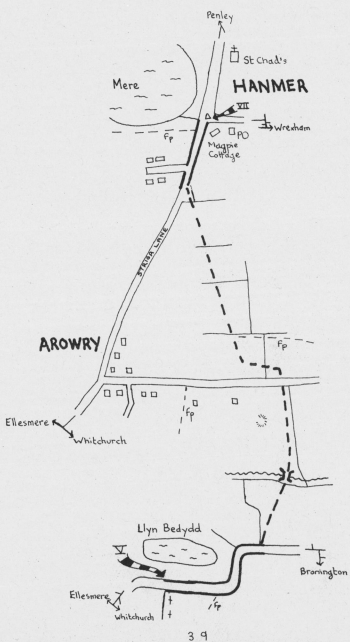

points of interest

[19] The name Llyn Bedydd literally means baptism lake and there is a legend that St Chad baptised converts here, although it is possible that Bedydd is derived from 'bedw' the Welsh for birch. Considering the great number of Welsh place names and the strength of early Welsh Christianity the legend sounds quite feasible.

The Meres were formed at the end of the last ice age, only 10,000 - 15,000 years ago, when lumps of ice sank into the soft terminal moraines (earth and rock that had been carried along with the glaciers' movement and then deposited).

Pteridium aquilinum
BRACKEN

[20] This is known as Ystriga Lane. The name is said to come from 'ystrigol' (the opening) and another derivation of this may be an early Welsh name for Hanmer. In records dating back to Edward I, a 'Johannes deCreting' is mentioned living in 'Strogul' in 'Wallia' (Wales). Between the years 670 and 1170 the names 'Chadhull' (the village of St Chad) and 'Chatwaste' (Chad's moorland) were used and the name 'Chaddlehunt' (Chad's hunt) in 1043 possibly refers to an area near Hanmer.

In 1202 the area east of the River Dee, known as 'Malaur Saisnec', was granted to the convent at Valle Crucis. Later, in 1270, the four sons of Madoc ap Gruffydd, Prince of Powys and Lord of Castell Dinas Brân near Llangollen, conceded to their English mother, Lady Emma Audley, for the term of her life, all lands and tenements given to her by their father in 'Maelor Saesneg' (Saxon Maelor). These lands included the 'vill' of 'Hagneme'.

It has been suggested that the name Hanmer may come from a Saxon personal name 'Hagena' and 'mere', although there is also a possibility that it came from 'Havering' or 'Hafren' (the old name for the River Severn) and 'mere'. A tributary of the Severn rises two miles to the south and the mere may have been thought to be the Severn's source.

westwards HANMER to BROOK LANE

A circular walk starting beside the mere is described on page 102.
The Maelor Way continues through Hanmer. Fork left at the
junction by a black and white cottage [21]. A right turn
will take you to the village shop and the Village Arms Hotel for
a wide variety of food and refreshment. Pass the church [22]
and a lane on your right leading to the village school [23]. Note
the staddle-stones [24] in the yard of a farm on your right.

Take the next stiles on your right and follow the left-hand
boundary. Beside you is Mere House [25] a private residence.
Walkers will notice another red horsechestnut tree in spring.
Two more stiles take you through a shelter belt of fir trees.
Proceed to the bypass and, directly opposite, find another
stile which leads you along the right-hand boundary of
two fields to Brook Lane. Turn left.

eastwards BROOK LANE to HANMER

In the field beside Brook Lane, follow the left-hand boundary.
Continue through another field to the Hanmer Bypass. Find
the stile opposite and go straight ahead using two stiles
to pass through a shelter belt of fir trees. Follow the
right-hand boundary to the road. A variety of trees grow
beside Mere House [25] a private residence to your right.

Turn left, noting the staddle-stones [24] in the yard of a farm
on your left. Pass the next lane on your left which leads to
Hanmer school [23]. Beyond the church [22], fork right at
the junction. A left turn here will lead you to the village
shop and the Village Arms Hotel where you can obtain a
wide variety of food and refreshment. Opposite the black
and white cottage [21] is a path beside the mere, part of
the circular route described on page 102.

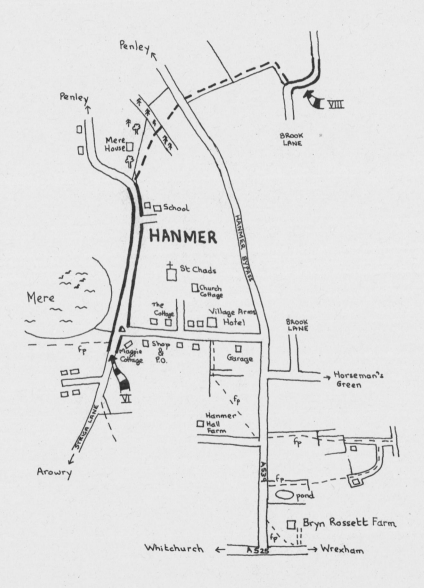

points of interest

[21] This dates from Tudor times and was once just known as 'The Cottage', later becoming known as 'Magpie Cottage'. Wattle and daub were used in its construction.

MAGPIE COTTAGE

[22] St Chad's has an interesting history. The original church may have been attached to the monastery at Bangor. Twelve hundred of the two thousand monks were put to death by Ethelfrith, King of Northumbria around 615 AD. Later, Leofric, Earl of Mercia gave St Chad's to the newly founded monastery in Coventry. In the twelfth century the Normans granted the church to Haughmond Abbey in Shropshire.

During the 13th century it is said that a hermit had himself bricked up in a cell here with only a hole for food, drink and confession. Owain Glyndwr [26] was married at St Chad's in the 14th century. Later on, in 1463, the church burnt down and was not rebuilt until 1490.

A preaching cross stands to the south of the church. In 1643, during the Civil War while the Hanmer family was fighting for the King, it was knocked down by the Parliamentarians, whilst in 1739 '10s 2d' (51p) was paid 'for setting ye cros stright'. In the north wall is the 'founder's tomb' said to be a memorial to the architect of the previous church who fell from the belltower during construction.

In 1714 a messenger interrupted Sir Thomas Hanmer during the service to tell him of Queen Anne's death Sir Thomas was the Speaker in Parliament.

CHURCHYARD CROSS
East Face
(from an engraving)

A chancery within the last church was built in 1720 and it was probably at this time that Robert Davies of Croesfoel near Wrexham was commissioned to produce the chancel gates, now the churchyard gates. Davies also produced other famous gates in the area including those at Chirk Castle mentioned in section XVI. The church bells were recast in 1778 for the old church and, in 1878, rehung. The village stocks remained in front of the church until 1868.

On 3rd February 1889, after Sunday morning service, the large church burnt down again, probably as a result of a fire spreading from the heating system. The Reverend Lee (who also wrote at least two volumes of notes on the history of Hanmer) saved some of the church registers from the blaze. Six new bells, the largest weighing 771 kilos (15cwt), were

made for a new church in 1890; the new building was designed by
Sir John Hanmer.

ST CHAD'S

[23] Hanmer School was set up by charitable endowment from a
bequest of 100 marks by Roger Billings in 1625. The oldest part of
the school was built in 1676 and is listed for preservation.
A government inspection during 1847 showed only 8 children
present in the 'neglected' and 'damp' building, although there
were 200 children in the area. It would appear that children
were kept away because of the poor conditions and because
the 60 year old 'untrained' master was too 'harsh'.

[24] Circles of staddle-stones once supported wooden platforms
on which hay ricks were built. The air gap
under the ricks prevented the crop being
spoilt by damp, and the build up of
inflammable gas. Rats could not climb up the
mushroom-shaped stones into the hay.
Nowadays the stones are collectors' items

STADDLE-STONE

for sale at antique shops, and their demand has created
the concrete staddle-stone. Complete with cracks and marks,
these imitations will easily fool the unwary.

[25] Mere House is a listed building and part of the
Hanmer Estate. The Hanmer family have been residents
of the village since the time of Henry III when the
lordship of the parish was given to them. The family
may also be descended from Thomas de Macclesfield who
was granted local wasteland by the freeholders of
Hanmer in 1284. The first recorded use of Hanmer as
a surname was in 1371 but the user may not have been
related to the later lord. The lordship passed through
Sir John Hanmer, and Sir Philip to Sir David, father-in-law
of Owain Glyndwr.

Hanmer Hall, on the other side of the village, was
originally built for Sir Thomas Hanmer between 1510
and 1545. It was taken by Parliament in the Civil War
while the Hanmers fought for the King. John Hanmer
became captain of a footsoldiers' company at York in
1642 while Sir Thomas warranted to raise archers, and
then 200 dragoniers in Nottingham.

The Hearth Roll of 1662, the forerunner of housing
rates (based on accommodation size) and the Community
Charge (based on number of residents), records 83 hearths
in the village; 12 in the home of Sir John Hanmer
but only one in many other dwellings. The present
Hall is the result of a rebuild for Sir Humphrey Hanmer
in the mid-18th century.

In 1773 the estate was inherited by Walden Hanmer of
Buckinghamshire who claimed title to about 600 hectares under an Inclosure Act. The Act no doubt increased
the agricultural value of the land which, once enclosed,

was improved for farming, but nowadays we might be concerned about the devastation of several wetlands through drainage. The lord, the vicar and other landowners took the local common land of Tallarn Green, Rosspoeth Green, Bronington Green, Little Green, Dorcross Green and Horsemoss (Horseman's) Green while, as usual, it is likely that the poorer inhabitants without holdings suffered by losing their grazing rights.

The tenants of local farms already had their tithes to pay :

> For every Cow a penny
> Every Calf a halfpenny
> Every Colt fourpence
> Eggs are in kind
> Every Hen two eggs and Cock three eggs
> Honey the tenth part due in kind or money to the value of the honey
> Geese in kind are due at seven, eight, nine and ten.

THE COTTAGE, HANMER

One of several listed buildings (all private residences) that can be found in the village.

[26] Several years after his marriage to Sir David Hanmer's daughter, Owain Glyndwr led the Welsh rebellion. Henry IV's forces were pushed into England but returned to crush the rebels. Sir David's son, John was fined 100 marks (about £67) for helping Owain. However, the Welsh rose again under Glyndwr's leadership and held their own parliament at Machynlleth. It was not until Prince Henry (later Henry V) led the English that the rebels were finally subjugated. Owain Glyndwr was never found.

SEAL OF
OWAIN GLYNDWR

westwards BROOK LANE to PENLEY

Head west along Brook Lane and fork left at the next
junction. At a right bend go ahead down a green track.
The hedgerows [27] along this section support many
climbing plants [28] and the track has an unusual
species for this area : hop [29].

At the lane go ahead and over a cross-road. In 400
metres use the stile on the right and bear left from
this to another lane. From the stile almost opposite
veer half-right to a bridge at the foot of the field.
From here continue ahead, keeping ponds on your right
in the next field and the third field ahead. Beyond a
stream, in sight of the houses, you turn left before a
fence and right to the estate. Bear right in front of
the houses, then left to the main road. Turn left.

Opposite the Post Office turn right into the Ellesmere road.

eastwards PENLEY to BROOK LANE

At the main road, opposite the Post Office, turn left. After
200 metres, beyond the houses, turn right and right again
through the housing estate. Look for a stile at the end
of a path on your left to enter the fields. Turn right
to the next stile then follow the boundary to your left.
Beyond the next stile go straight ahead over stiles, bridges
and through bridlegates. In the sixth field, beyond the
second gated bridge, you need to veer half-right to the
lane after climbing a bank.

A stile to your left takes you, veering right, across the
field to a lane. Turn left and after 400 metres go ahead
over the cross-road and, at the left bend, stay ahead
up a green track. The hedgerows [27] along this

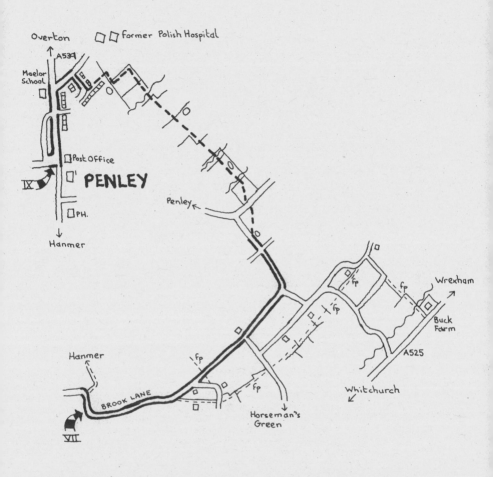

section support many climbing plants **[28]** and this track
has an unusual species for this area: hop **[29]**.

At the lane continue ahead and ignore the next left.
In 800 metres, at the sharp left bend, the Way continues
over a stile beside the gate on your right.

points of interest

[27] During the 1970's a formula for dating hedgerows was developed in southern England by Dr Max Hooper of the Nature Conservancy Council. A simplified version of this formula is that in a 30 metre length of hedgerow each constituent species equals 100 years in the life of the hedge, ie:

Hedge age = species per 30 metres × 100

Ulmus glabra
WYCH ELM

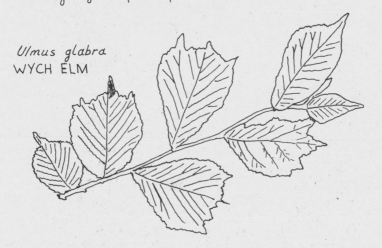

It must now be said that this technique of dating is not as precise as was first suggested. For example, along one old road in Wrexham Maelor, a species count differs along various sections of the hedge. Where cattle have been grazing there are only 4 or 5 species in 30 metres whilst other sections reveal 10 species giving calculated age differences of over 500 years.

However, species counts can still be a pointer towards hedgerow dating. Hedges with more than 4 species may have been planted before the 18th century Inclosure Acts. Species-rich hedges especially those with ancient woodland indicators such as field maple and guelder rose tend to be even older. Try estimating the ages of some hedgerows on the Maelor Way especially if you have children with you.

[28] The plants shown on this page are used in hedgerow 'age estimations'.

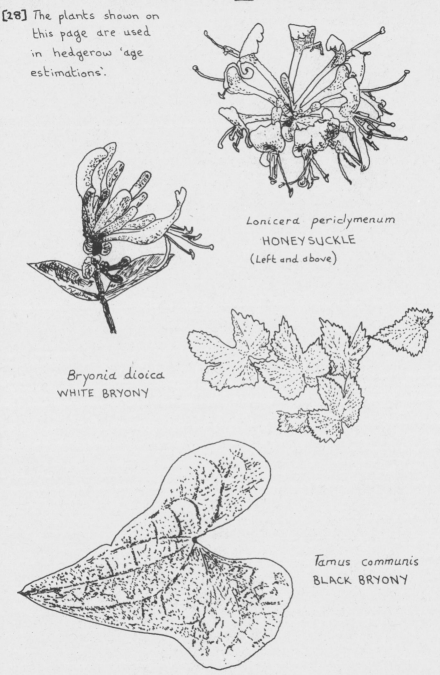

Lonicera periclymenum
HONEYSUCKLE
(Left and above)

Bryonia dioica
WHITE BRYONY

Tamus communis
BLACK BRYONY

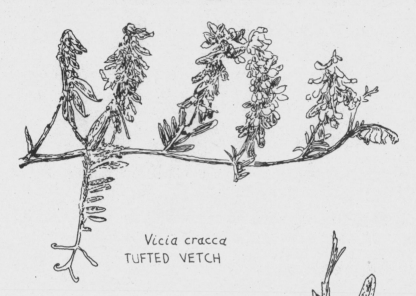

Vicia cracca
TUFTED VETCH

Vicia sepium
BUSH VETCH

Geranium robertianum
HERB-ROBERT

The plants shown on this
page are not normally
used for hedge-dating as
they are also found in
meadows and on waste
ground.

Pyronia tithonus
GATEKEEPER

Almost at its northern limit, this butterfly depends on hedgerows and woodland margins and is sometimes known as the 'hedge brown'. It is fond of bramble flowers.

Humulus lupus
HOP

[29] Hop plants are not often seen in the Wrexham Maelor area although a farm accounts book of 1644 found in Hanmer lists hops and flax as major crops. The plants in this hedgerow are possibly the last survivors of that arable crop which, no doubt, was grown for its traditional use: flavouring beer with the female flowers. Herbally the plant is a sedative used to treat insomnia; one more good reason why beer should not be drunk before driving.

westwards PENLEY to CROSS MILL

Follow the Ellesmere Road opposite the Post Office and after 200 metres take the path on your right beyond 'Rose Cottage'. Cross two fields using the bridge in between. In the next field turn right and follow the boundary to the hollow of a former pond. Turn left and head alongside the ditch to cross a private driveway and veer slightly left in the fields beyond. Use two gates to continue in the same direction. Descend and turn right beyond the next gate to follow the course of a disused mill-leat but cut off the corner. Beyond a partly-stone stile at the end of the field, go through a small field, the site of the former corn mill, into a large yard. Turn right.   Go through a gate and ascend to a stile on the left; from this go ahead to the road. Cross the bridge and take the stile beside it. The Way now goes ahead through four fields following the vaguely discernable, disused mill-leat. At the farm track turn left.

eastwards CROSS MILL to PENLEY

Follow the concrete drive to the stile on the right. Cross three fields on the same contour. This path was the former course of a mill-leat. In the fourth field head slightly left for the concrete bridge. At the road turn left. Take the path in the layby on the right. From the gate go ahead through the farm. In the next field head down to buildings. The Way goes through a large yard and turns through a gate opposite the cottage.   Head slightly left through the field, the site of the former corn mill, to a partly-stone stile. Now follow the mill-leat around the field but cut off the corner. Take the second gate on your left and head uphill. Use two gates at the top to continue in roughly the same direction but veering left to stiles leading across a private driveway.   Follow the ditch toward the fence opposite but turn right before it. At the next field corner cross the stile. Go over to the protruding field corner then follow the right-hand boundary. From the bridge go ahead to the lane and turn left into Penley village.

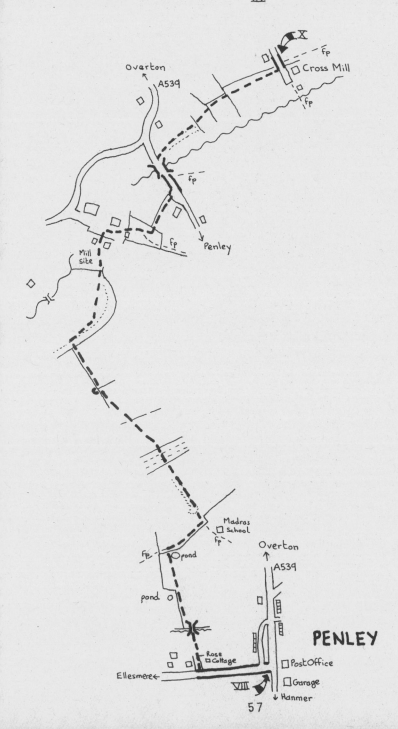

X

FP

Cross Mill

FP

Overton
A539

fp

fp

Penley

Mill
site

Madras
School

fp

fp

FP

pond

Overton

A539

pond

PENLEY

Post Office

Rose
Cottage

Garage

Ellesmere←

VIII

↓Hanmer

X

westwards CROSS MILL to OVERTON

Turn right at the lane and take the first stile on your left. Follow the left-hand field boundary, then the woodland boundary to a bridlegate. Go through the wood, crossing the stream. In the next field stay by the left-hand boundary, then use the stile but continue ahead. At the lane turn left and take the first path on your right. Beyond the dismantled railway [30] bear slightly left and enter the woodland through a bridlegate.

Descend into the valley then climb to the farm, Plas yn Coed. Beyond the first gate, turn left and, after the next, turn right to reach and cross the driveway. Beyond the next valley, rise to cross a stile and turn left. Go ahead across a third valley and over two stiles. Turn left to another. Head for the far corner of this long field then turn left to reach an enclosed path which leads around Overton School.

eastwards OVERTON to CROSS MILL

Follow the path around Overton School. In the field, follow the right-hand boundary for 300 metres to cross a stile and another in the far corner of the long field. Go ahead to use a stile on your right and cross the breadth of the field to another. Now go straight ahead into the valley through the gateway, and then ascend to a stile in the right-hand boundary. After another valley and another gateway you reach the gate outside Plas yn Coed. Go through the gate opposite and skirt the fence to enter via the next gate. Go through another gate, on your right by the farmyard, and head straight across the field and down into the valley. After the bridge ascend the woodland path, taking a left fork near the top and going through a bridlegate. Head slightly left to cross a dismantled railway [30] and reach the lane. Turn left to take the next stile on your right. Proceed using another stile but continue in the same direction to enter woodland. ↗

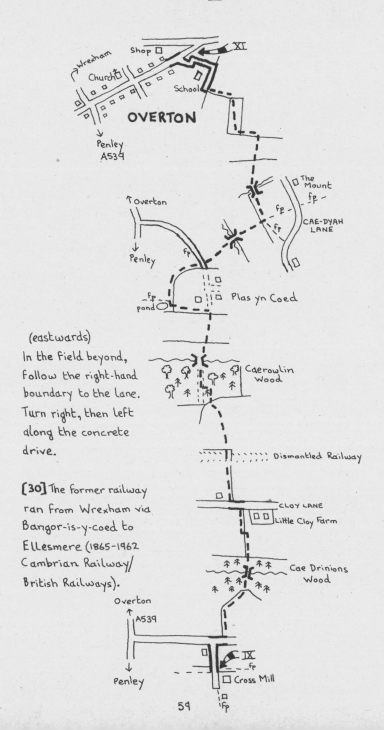

XI

↗ Wrexham   Shop 🔲

Church ✝   🔲 🔲 🔲

School

OVERTON

↓ Penley
A539

↑ Overton

↓ Penley

🔲 The Mount
fp
fp
fp   CAE-DYAH
LANE

fp
pond ○   🔲 Plas yn Coed

(eastwards)

In the field beyond, follow the right-hand boundary to the lane. Turn right, then left along the concrete drive.

Caerowlin Wood

Dismantled Railway

[30] The former railway ran from Wrexham via Bangor-is-y-coed to Ellesmere (1865-1962 Cambrian Railway/ British Railways).

🔲   CLOY LANE
🔲 🔲 Little Cloy Farm

Cae Drinions Wood

Overton
↑ A539

↓ Penley

IX
fp

🔲 Cross Mill

fp

westwards OVERTON to SHELL BROOK

At the road turn left *unless you wish to visit the shop by turning right then left.* The Maelor Way now goes ahead to the main crossroad and turns right to a lane on the bend *but you may wish to look around the village* [31] *and refresh yourself before you continue.*

Descend the lane to reach a large field: a flood plain and former loop of the Dee. Head along the embankment path to the riverside then turn left. After about 400 metres enter the woodland [32] and follow the riverside path through woods and small fields eventually reaching a set of steps that once served a ferry [33] to the Boat Inn [34] and Erbistock Church [35]. Those who did not refresh themselves at Overton may now be regretting the ferry's closure.

Continue along the riverside path and, at the top of the steep slope, fork right and descend to the footbridge over Shell Brook.

eastwards SHELL BROOK to OVERTON

Beyond the footbridge, climb the slope and fork left to stay on the riverside path. Opposite Erbistock Church [35] and the Boat Inn [34] is a set of steps that once served the ferry [33]. Beyond the woods [32] and small fields you reach a large field: a flood plain and former loop of the river. After about 400 metres fork right along the embankment toward higher land. Cross two stiles and follow the lane uphill.

The Maelor Way turns right at the main road then left at the crossroad. You may wish to have a look around the village [31] or refresh yourself before you continue. Proceed to the village school.

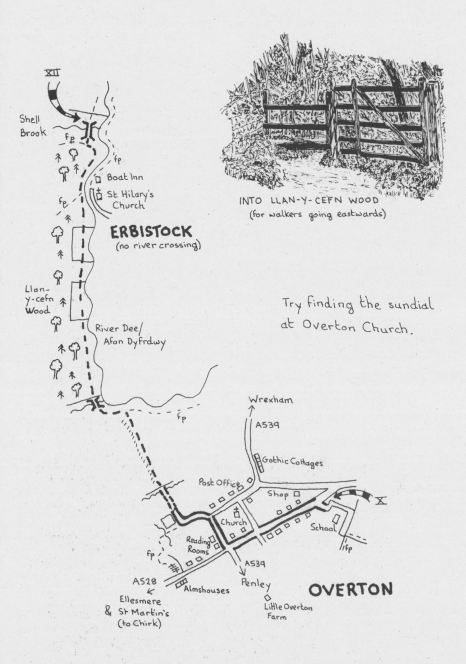

XII

Shell Brook

fp

Boat Inn

St Hilary's Church

ERBISTOCK
(no river crossing)

Llan-y-cefn Wood

fp

River Dee/ Afon Dyfrdwy

fp

INTO LLAN-Y-CEFN WOOD
(for walkers going eastwards)

Try finding the sundial at Overton Church.

Wrexham

A539

Gothic Cottages

Post Office

Shop

X

Church

School

Reading Rooms

fp

fp

A539

Penley

OVERTON

A528

Almshouses

Ellesmere & St Martin's (to Chirk)

Little Overton Farm

points of interest

[31] The name Overton probably comes from the Saxon meaning 'upper settlement'; the village is built on a headland of red sandstone. After the Norman invasion it was granted to Robert Fitzhugh. During the twelfth century it was owned by the Welsh Prince of Powys who founded Valle Crucis Abbey near Llangollen. On his death it was given to his son Madoc ap Gruffydd (ap = son of).

After the Welsh annexation to England, Edward I bestowed it on his queen, Eleanor, who gave it to Robert de Creve Coeure. Edward granted the village a market in 1286 and six years later it became a free borough. All this, no doubt, to encourage English residents and strengthen the border.

The year 1307 saw Edward II bestow Overton on his queen, Isobel, and in 1347 Edward III gave it to Eirbule le Strange, Baron of Knockys. Henry IV gave Overton to Sir John Stanley and the family held it from 1400 to 1599.

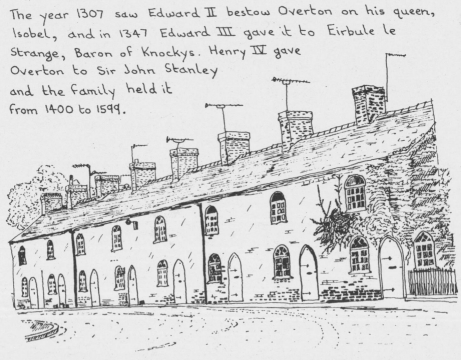

19TH CENTURY 'GOTHIC' COTTAGES : WREXHAM ROAD

BRYN-Y-PYS MANSION (now demolished)

More recently, much of the land and buildings in Overton have been owned by the Bryn-y-pys (hill of peas) Estate after being handed down through the Price family and then sold to Edmund Ethelston, who changed his name to Peel after the purchase. The Peel family lived in a large Georgian mansion on the northern edge of the village until 1955 when the deteriorating building was demolished. A gatehouse and the parkland containing mature trees can be seen along the Wrexham Road while the names of Peel and Bryn-y-pys reoccur throughout the village and in the church. Many of the oak stiles that unfortunately had to be replaced on the Maelor Way were erected by the estate as far as Penley. Some still remain overgrown in the hedgerow beside the new stiles and bear carved dates of around 1905.

The late 19th century 'Cocoa and Reading Rooms' were built by Edmund Peel to try to discourage drunkenness in the village.

The present church building was restored in 1870 but an earlier building here was referred to as a chapel in 1402. One of the church bells dates from 1615 and the pulpit has been dated to 1637. A pamphlet on the church is available inside.

The church is famous for its yew trees, one of the seven wonders of Wales:

> Pistyll Rhaeadr and Wrexham steeple,
> Snowdon's mountain without its people,
> Overton yew-trees, St Winifrede's wells,
> Llangollen bridge, and Gresford bells.

YEW TREE

A tollbar on the former turnpike road was situated near the present police station. Records for the Shrewsbury to Wrexham turnpike in 1752 show that a penny was charged for any 'Horse, Mare, Gelding, Mule, or Ass laden or unladen and not drawing in any carriage'. The salary of Edward Teggin, the tollgate keeper, was 8 shillings a week. Compare this with the 1771 wage of 'John Williams, Collector of the Tolls at Bronygarth gate' (on the Wem turnpike): '4s a week', 'provided that his weekly receipt amounts to that sum, otherwise he must be satisfied wth such deficient sum as he shall receive?.

Before the 17th century many British roads were in a terrible state. In order to improve them the first Turnpike Act of 1663 was followed by many others in the early 18th century. The toll-roads were controlled by Turnpike Trusts who charged a toll at gates or bars along the routes. The improvement of these roads created their own form of genius in roadbuilding techniques : John Metcalf (1717-1810) a blind man who started laying stone sets with chippings to fill in cracks ; John Macadam (1756-1836) whose method was to lay only local large stone covered by graduatingly smaller stone (he never used tarmacadam as is popularly believed); and Thomas Telford (1757-1837) who built the London to Holyhead road.

Even so, not all roads were kept in good condition, and not everyone wanted to pay the toll. This resulted in overland drovers' roads avoiding the tollgates and also in the 'pikes' on top of the gates to prevent horsemen jumping over, whilst in North Wales the 'Rebecca' movement had men disguised as women trying to wreck the gates.

These factors helped to cause the eventual dismantling of the turnpikes so that by the end of the 19th century most roads were repaired by the county councils and the age of the toll-roads had virtually ended. However, milestones and the former toll-houses, which usually had a protruding room with views of the traffic from both directions, can still be found. There is a former toll-house north of Chirk village, another near Glyndyfrdwy, one east of Mold, and a complete rebuild with gates at the Ironbridge Gorge Museum.

[32] Llan-y-cefn (church ridge) wood is rich in wildlife. Spring walkers will see snowdrop, ramsons, wood anemone, bluebell and marsh marigold as well as common dog-violet, dog's-mercury and yellow archangel.

In summer the dense overhead foliage keeps the lower vegetation from becoming too overgrown and the difficulties of harvesting timber here have created an ecosystem where dead trees decay on the woodland floor supporting insects and fungi. Mycologists can look out for jew's ear, scarlet elf cup, candlesnuff fungus and a variety of polypores.

Allium ursinum

THE SEMITRANSPARENT
FLOWER SHEATH OF
RAMSONS

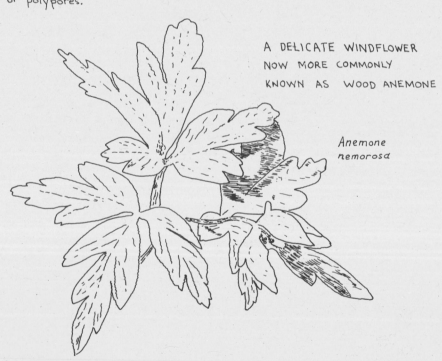

A DELICATE WINDFLOWER
NOW MORE COMMONLY
KNOWN AS WOOD ANEMONE

Anemone nemorosa

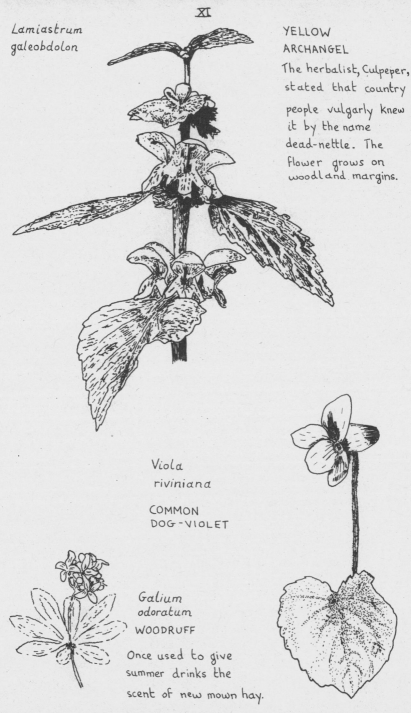

Lamiastrum galeobdolon

YELLOW ARCHANGEL
The herbalist, Culpeper, stated that country people vulgarly knew it by the name dead-nettle. The flower grows on woodland margins.

Viola riviniana

COMMON DOG-VIOLET

Galium odoratum
WOODRUFF

Once used to give summer drinks the scent of new mown hay.

KINGFISHER
Alcedo attis

from a wood engraving by Fussell
and Thompson 1840.

The area on both
sides of the Dee
is mentioned in
the RSPB Guide
to Birdwatching
in Clwyd but
two birds sometimes
spotted here, the
cormorant and the
kingfisher, are not listed.

Mercurialis
perennis

DOG'S MERCURY
from an 1808 engraving.

The green leaves
of this plant
can be found
in Llan-y-cefn
wood throughout
the year. Male
and female
plants grow
seperately.

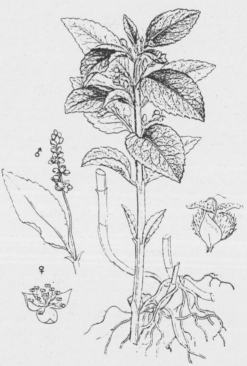

[33] The ferry, which ceased operation in 1939, was a small boat pulled across by a winch on the far bank. In 1896 over ten thousand passengers crossed the river here. Those who are really thirsty might try to paddle across the Dee in summer, the old ford lies diagonally under the water.

THE
BOAT
INN

[34] The Boat Inn is advertised on approach roads as the '16th Century Boat Inn', although one writer claims that the inn was formerly workers' cottages and that the licence was not obtained until 1857.

[35] St Hilary's Church stands on a site that was used, in 1291, as a rectory. This is at least the third church here; the present building was completed in 1861 while the former building stood from 1778 to 1849. The earliest was recorded in 1692.

ST HILARY'S CHURCH
ERBISTOCK

westwards SHELL BROOK to FLANNOG FARM

Continue alongside the Dee through one field <u>then drop down to the riverside path.</u> At the lane turn left and left again at the next junction. Beside a timber-framed building [38] fork right and follow the enclosed track [37] for a kilometre. (Do not take gates on the right or left.) At one point the track opens out into a field but continues on the far side.

Across the river is Pen-y-lan [36]. At the junction turn right and keep the farmhouse to your right. The house probably dates from the 16th century and is listed for preservation.

Go through the woodland and, in the meadow beyond – at the first corner, continue slightly right and ascend to a stile at the top of the field. After the next stile go ahead beside Flannog Farm.

eastwards FLANNOG FARM to SHELL BROOK

Continue past Flannog Farm and take the signed path on the corner, veering half-right across another stile and down to the green track at the foot of the meadow. Continue in the same direction. Spring walkers may notice the pink hawthorn just before the gate: the flower colour is a result of a cross between the red midland hawthorn and our common variety. Look to your left to see Pen-y-lan [36].

Follow the track through the wood and beside Plas-yn-y-coed (hall in the wood). The house may date from the 16th century and is listed for preservation. At the lane turn left. After about a kilometre the track [37] is broken by a field but continues on the far side. At the T-junction, by a timber-framed farm [38], turn left. →

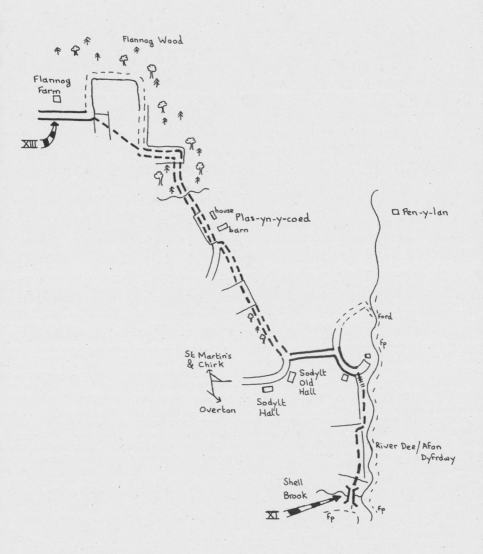

At the next junction turn right and beyond the farm, at
the end of the track, take the riverside path on the right.
In the field, continue in the same direction to reach a
footbridge over Shell Brook.

points of interest

[36]

PEN-Y-LAN

Pen-y-lan (from pen=top y=of the llan=church land) is referred to in 'Buildings of Wales: Clwyd' by Edward Hubbard. The original house is said to date from 1690 and was remodelled, stuccoed and castellated in 1830. A 19th century owner built a private chapel nearby and that is now the village church.

[37] Although this track is a public road, it is little used except by farmers, occasional horseriders and walkers. As a result a variety of plants and insects can be seen. In summer look out for butterflies — orange-tip and speckled wood.

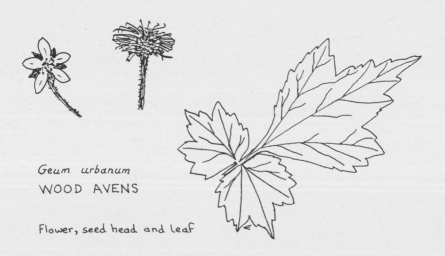

Geum urbanum
WOOD AVENS

Flower, seed head and leaf

Pararge aegeria
SPECKLED WOOD BUTTERFLY

Vicia sepium
BUSH VETCH

Seed pods

Alliaria petiolata
GARLIC MUSTARD

A food plant of the
orange-tip butterfly.
Anthocharis cardamines

[38] This timber-framed farmhouse is Sodylt Old Hall. The central part of the building is a cruck-built hall possibly dating to the 14th century. Along the lane is the larger Sodylt Hall.

SODYLT OLD HALL

The earliest records found to date relating to 'Sodylt' appear in a deed between 'Roger Jennings of Sodylt in the township of Dudleston, Gentleman,' and Richard Chambre of Bolton, together with John Chambre of Bolton concerning lands for a pre-nuptial settlement of Roger Jennings and Margaret Chambre. In 1795 'Sodyllt Hall' was auctioned. Unfortunately early records do not make the individual properties clear; there are at least four by the name of Sodylt on this lane.

A TYPICAL CRUCK FRAMEWORK

Two main curved timbers support roof.

S A L O P.

A PARTICULAR
AND CONDITIONS OF SALE
OF SEVERAL ESTATES

Let at the Yearly Rent of £450, or thereabouts,

Situate in the Township of DUDLESTONE, in the Parish of ELLESMERE, in the County of SALOP;

Which, by the Direction of the Trustees named in an Act of Parliament, ARE

To be SOLD by Public Auction,

By Mr. PRICKETT,

At the Royal Oak, in Ellesmere,

On WEDNESDAY, the 20th Day of MAY, 1795,

AT ONE O'CLOCK.

LOT I.

A Substantial and Handsome Brick MANSION HOUSE, called SODDYLT HALL; the same consisting of five rooms on the attic story, four good bed-chambers on the first floor, with a handsome principal and back staircase, two good parlours, a hall, kitchens, and extensive dry cellaring under the house; a large garden and fore court included with a brick wall and pallisadoes, and sundry offices, viz. a brew-house, dairy, malt-house or a hop-house, with a good kiln, two store rooms, a barn, good stabling, cow-houses, and other necessary buildings, together with the several fields or Pieces of Land hereinafter mentioned, containing the several quantities following, or thereabout, viz.

	Quality of the Land	Particular Contents A. R. P.	Total Contents A. R. P.
The Garden, Fore Court, &c. contains	—		0 0 12
The Orchard	—	Pasture 0 2 2	
Kiln Meadow	—	Meadow 3 2 24	
Carried over			6 0 06

(2)

	Quality of the Land	Particular Contents A. R. P.	Total Contents A. R. P.
Brought over			6 0 38
Two Mill Pieces	Meadow	1 0 3	
	Wood	1 0 16	
Withy Coppice	Wood	0 2 33	
The Hop Yard Piece	Meadow and Hops	3 0 15	
The Hop Yard Coppice	Meadow and Wood	6 3 32	
Orchard Croft	Arable	1 0 13	
Hall Field	Ditto	7 1 36	
Stoney Croft	Ditto	0 3 39	
Bellin a Cowws Coppice	Wood	4 1 1	
Pigeon House Field*	Meadow	3 2 18	
Brick Kiln Field	Ditto	4 1 8	
Crooked Field	Pasture	7 1 29	
Far Patch	Ditto	4 2 0	
Crab Mill Meadow	Wood	0 0 34	
Jenny Lee's Croft	Meadow	6 0 8	
	Ditto	1 2 4	

* In this Field there is a holy well, with brick Pigeon House.

The Mansion House and Lands before mentioned, except the Woodlands, which are in hand, are in the occupation of Mr. John George, as Tenant for a Year from Lady-day last.

Also TWO TENEMENTS or COTTAGES, formerly one Tenement, and called Parbotts, with three Gardens, now in the occupation of Richard Owen and Edward White, as Tenants for a year from Lady-day last. The gardens contain about — 0 1 21

Also a brick DWELLING-HOUSE, with a SMITH's-SHOP and Garden, now in the occupation of Joseph Owens, as tenant for a year from Lady-day last. The Garden contains about — 0 0 18

Also a PEW near the middle of the South Gallery in ELLESMERE CHURCH.

Also a large PEW on the South Side of DUDLESTONE CHAPEL, being the one nearest the Altar.

Making together | | | 59 0 8

The underwood in the several pieces of Land called Mill Piece, Withy Coppice, Hop-Yard Coppice, Bellin-a-Cowws Coppice, and Far-Patch, with the timber trees and saplings standing on all the Lands comprised in Lot 1, have been valued by a surveyor, and estimated worth £.754 13 8 and which sum is therefore to be paid by the purchaser of this Lot, exclusive of and besides the sum he shall bid for the Estate.

There is a small Rent of 4s. 6d. per Annum issuing out of Soddylt Estate, payable to the Earl of Powis, and the Estate comprised in this Lot is sold subject thereto.

LOT

AUCTION PARTICULARS 1795

westwards FLANNOG FARM to GLYNMORLAS

At the first junction fork right and go along the open track to a T-junction. Turn right and immediately take the stile on your right. Keep the boundary to your left then, in the next field [39] bear half-left to reach the lane. In the next field, beyond the steps, follow the woodland boundary, crossing more stiles. After a stile beside a gate, drop down onto the woodland path. Ignore a fork to the right but continue to a stile leading you onto a lane [40] by 'Woodside'.

In spring, comfrey growing on the verges at the foot of this lane attracts bumble bees [41] and moths. At the road junction, beyond Glenbrook Cottage, go straight ahead. This road was once part of a route for miners going to Black Park Colliery near Chirk and was known locally as 'Cat's Walk'.

eastwards GLYNMORLAS to FLANNOG FARM

This road was once trodden by miners going to Black Park Colliery near Chirk and was known locally as 'Cat's Walk'. Fork right at the junction to keep Glenbrook Cottage on the left. In spring, comfrey growing on the verges attracts bumble bees [41] and moths. At the head of the lane [40] beyond 'Woodside', turn left, then right beyond the stile to follow the path through Bramble Wood. Do not take the first stile on your right but fork right to cross one beside a gate. Continue along the woodland boundary, crossing two more stiles then veering right to the lane. After the steps, in the next field [39] go half-right to a stile on the right-hand boundary. Continue ahead to the lane. Turn left and immediately left again. Look to your left for a good view along the Vale of Llangollen to Llantysilio Mountain. Follow the lane (soon a track) to a T-junction and bear left to pass Flannog Farm.

GLYNMORLAS

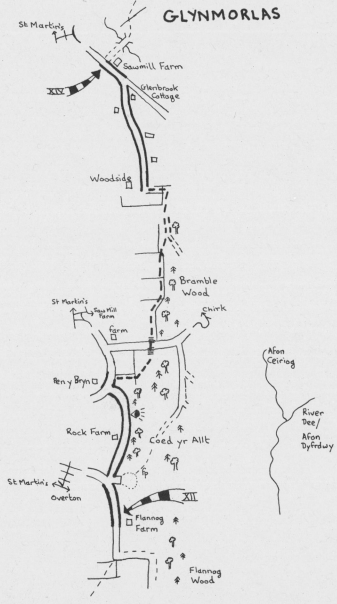

St Martin's

Sawmill Farm

XIV

Glenbrook Cottage

Woodside

Bramble Wood

St Martin's

Saw Mill Farm

Chirk

farm

Afon Ceiriog

Pen y Bryn

Rock Farm

Coed yr Allt

River Dee / Afon Dyfrdwy

St Martin's

Overton

XII

Flannog Farm

Flannog Wood

points of interest

[39] The tithe map of 1838 records the name of this field as Cae Ffynon, Welsh for well field. Welsh and English names can be found all over the Marches: the border country where British (ie Welsh) kingdoms were conquered first by the Saxons and later by the Normans. The borders changed so often, even after Offa had built his dyke, that the Norman Marcher lords only had their boundaries set on the English side and were free to hold whatever land they could defend and maintain on the Welsh side.

[40] A story has been related to me about the long cottage on the brow of the hill. Apparently, a former owner bought a piglet and kept it for some time. Eventually deciding that the, now larger, pig should become bacon, he asked a friend to help him butcher it. His friend was to cut its throat while the owner sat on its back and held its ears. However, when the knife appeared, the pig, which perhaps realised that there was an ulterior motive for its owner's friendship and all those tasty meals it had been receiving, gave a loud squeal and headed off, dumping its treacherous owner in the stream on the way.

CARTOON
by Brian Walker

Reproduced with his permission from the October/November 1990 issue of The Countryman.

'Ar — I minds when us used ter kill the pigs in wot you calls yer lounge, hanged 'em in yer bedroom and scalded 'em in yer dinin' room . . .'

[41] There are seven major species of bumble bee in Britain, their stripes or bands varying with white, yellow, orange, gold and black colouration. Their annual colonies, formed in nests of grass and moss, often inhabit well-drained earth banks. They produce about a hundred workers which collect nectar and pollen to rear the young. Later in the year the queen lays eggs which produce males and females. After pairing, the females hibernate for winter and form new colonies in spring.

Bombus pratorum
BUMBLE BEE (ON COMFREY)

Comfrey has an interesting history. Other names for the plant include boatman's cabbage, due to its profusion and use on canals, and knitbone, relating to the use of its root, dried and ground, as a plaster. The plant is used in natural remedies as it contains allantoin, a substance which stimulates cell proliferation and helps wounds to heal. In his herbal, Culpeper recommended that the root boiled in water or wine, and the decoction drank, heals inward hurts, bruises, wounds and ulcers of the lung.

Recent research has revealed that the plant also contains vitamin B12, which it absorbs from the excreta of earthworms, and may be the only vegetable source of this vitamin. Organic gardeners grow the plant as a 'green manure' because of its deep roots which bring up low level minerals and because it produces an enormous weight of green leaves each year (per acre), more than any other plant growing in Britain.

Symphytum officinale
COMFREY

79

westwards GLYNMORLAS to GLEDRID BRIDGE

Here there is a choice of routes across the valley: the Maelor Way goes right, through the gate immediately beyond Sawmill Farm. Follow the track over the River Ceiriog, taking the stile on your left and ascending to the next lane. An alternative route passing a listed building [42] can be made by continuing along the lane, ignoring left turns. Beyond the stone bridge over the Ceiriog, turn sharp right at the T-junction and cross the first stile on your left.

Both routes continue from here: cross the field ahead, skirting the pheasantry, then follow the field outside the woodland boundary to gates [43] on the right. Do not enter these but fork left across the fields of Rhyn Park [44] using the far stile in the first field. At the track go ahead and under the A5, then cross the road. Pass the New Inn to join the towpath below Gledrid Bridge.

eastwards GLEDRID BRIDGE to GLYNMORLAS

Turn left beside the New Inn. Cross the road and continue along the lane. Pass Gledrid Farm on your left and go under the A5; the Way now becomes a green track. At the T-junction, use the stile and go half-left across Rhyn Park [44]. When you reach the gates [43] leading into the wood turn half-right to stay outside the woodland boundary and skirt a pheasantry to reach the lane.

Here there is a choice of routes across the valley: the Maelor Way continues straight ahead and descends via the track to cross the river. On reaching another lane it turns left beside a building, Sawmill Farm. An alternative route passing a listed building [42] can be taken by turning right at the lane and sharp left at the first junction. In the valley cross the stone bridge, ignore turns to the right and you will reach Sawmill Farm.

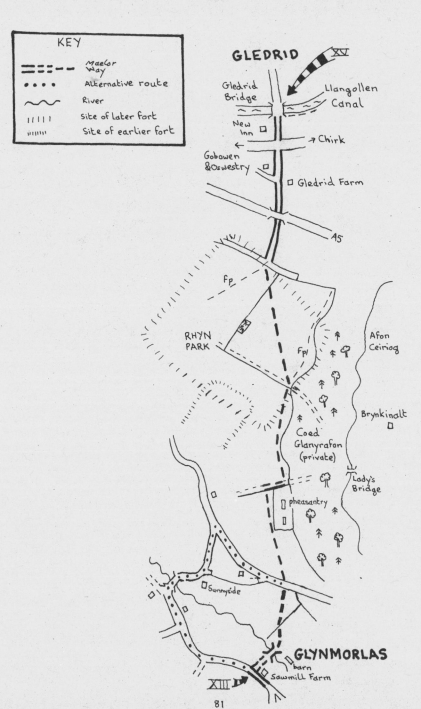

KEY

Maelor Way
Alternative route
River
Site of later fort
Site of earlier fort

GLEDRID

XV

Gledrid Bridge

Llangollen Canal

New Inn

→ Chirk

Gobowen & Oswestry

Gledrid Farm

A5

Fp

RHYN PARK

Fp/

Afon Ceiriog

Brynkinalt

Coed Glanyrafon (private)

Lady's Bridge

pheasantry

Sunnyside

GLYNMORLAS

barn
Sawmill Farm

XIII

points of interest

[42] Sunnyside is a 17th century timber-framed building on the alternative route.

SUNNYSIDE (Private residence)

[43] These gates are on the southern access road from Lord Trevor's house at Brynkinalt. The private road crosses the castellated Lady's Bridge (built for Lady Dungannon in the early 19th century) and heads for Bryn-y-gwyla Lodge (now disused). The site of Brynkinalt dates from at least the 10th century and has passed through the family to the present Lord. During the 15th century John ap David took the name Trevor from his ancestor, Tudor Trevor. The brick and stone front of the house dates from the early 17th century.

[44] Aerial photography in Britain has revealed a large number of prehistoric, Roman and Dark Age sites, giving us totally new ideas of both population levels and military activity and causing a drastic revision of our history books. Photographs of

crop markings taken during the drought of 1976 produced evidence of a Roman fort on this plain. Major rescue excavations on the site showed forts of two ages. Although the dates of these forts are uncertain it is believed that they predate Chester (DEVA) and that this was a major strategic base linked to Wroxeter (URICONIUM) via a marching camp at Whittington.

Roman records reveal that in AD 48 Ostorius Scapula led an expedition into the territory of the Deceangli whilst in AD 60 Suetonius Paullinus attacked North Wales and invaded Anglesey to wipe out the Druids. Later, during the years AD 77 and 78, Agricola carried out a successful campaign against the Ordovices of North Wales. The forts may have been built for one or more of these campaigns.

It is probable that the base was abandoned when the fortress at Chester was built. At the beginning of the 20th century, years before the fort's discovery, it was suggested that a Roman road followed the course of Stryt Yr Hwch in Sontley, near Wrexham. A line that leads directly from Rhyn Park to Chester via Pulford and Marford (where excavations in 1989 by John Dutton revealed two sections of road) include this 'Stryt'.

Another road, which appeared to researchers to leave the fort on the east side, may cross the Afon Ceiriog and go along the top of the hills above the Vale of Llangollen on its way to CAERHUN (a Roman fort in the Conwy valley).

BARN AT SAWMILL FARM

westwards GLEDRID BRIDGE to CHIRK BANK

From Gledrid, walkers may return along the Llangollen Canal towpath to Grindley Brook by turning left. Those who are continuing on the Maelor Way may still like to see the former wharf of the Glyn Valley Tramway [45] now just unusual bumps in a field about 300 metres along the canal to your left.

The Maelor Way goes along the towpath [46] to your right as far as the next bridge beside the post office at Chirk Bank. It runs parallel to the former A5 London-Holyhead road. The A5 now crosses the Ceiriog Viaduct [47] to your right.

Ahead, the towpath leads over the aqueduct [48] and through Chirk Tunnel [49]. On the road above the tunnel exit are, to the right, Chirk Castle Gates [54] and, to the left, Chirk Station and Village. (A road route avoiding the tunnel is given on the map.)

eastwards CHIRK BANK to GLEDRID BRIDGE

To your left, but not part of the Maelor Way, the towpath leads over the aqueduct [48] and through Chirk Tunnel [49]. On the road above the tunnel exit are, to your right, Chirk Castle Gates [54] and, to the left, Chirk Station and Village. (A road route avoiding the tunnel is given on the map.)

The Maelor Way goes along the canal towpath [46] to your right as far as the next bridge at Gledrid. It runs parallel to the former A5 London-Holyhead road. The A5 now crosses the Ceiriog Viaduct [47] to your left. From Gledrid, walkers can use the canal towpath to Grindley Brook and return on the Maelor Way or vice-versa.

Those who are not following the circular route may still like to see the former wharf of the Glyn Valley Tramway [45] now just unusual bumps in a field about 300 metres farther on.

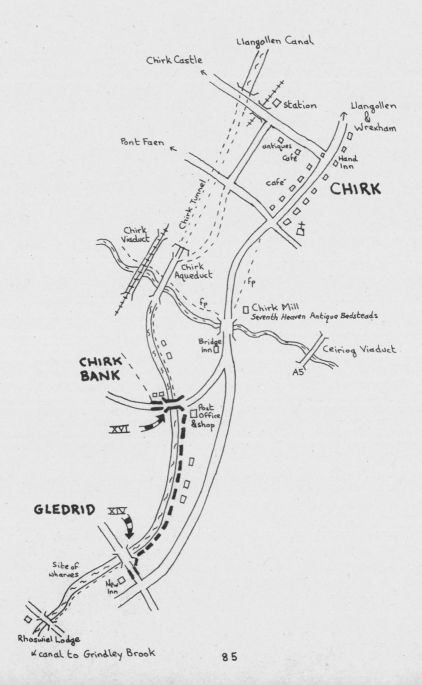

Llangollen Canal

Chirk Castle

station

Llangollen & Wrexham

Pont Faen

antiques café

café

Hand Inn

CHIRK

Chirk Tunnel

Chirk Viaduct

Chirk Aqueduct

fp

fp

Chirk Mill
Seventh Heaven Antique Bedsteads

CHIRK BANK

Bridge Inn

Ceiriog Viaduct

A5

XVI

Post Office & shop

GLEDRID

XIV

Site of wharves

New Inn

Rhoswiel Lodge

← canal to Grindley Brook

points of interest

[45] The Glyn Valley Tramway was designed to bring minerals from
Glyn Ceiriog to the canal where there were wharves and a basin,
now filled in. The eastern end of the line was adopted from the
Chirk Bank Colliery. Originally, the wagons were horsedrawn. Later
on, the route was altered, steam engines were introduced and
passengers were carried. The new line stayed on the Welsh bank
of the Afon Ceiriog, to meet the railway at Chirk Station (see map).

The tramway was unusual, not only with its ½ gauge but also in
that it ran alongside the turnpike road. Sir Theodore Martin –
biographer to Queen Victoria, and Henry Dennis – a famous local
brick manufacturer, were the main supporters of the venture.
Engines on the line were named after them.

Although the tramway became a tourist attraction in the early
20th century, the line closed for passengers in 1933 and for goods
in 1935.

[46] The canal here was relined with ferro-concrete during
the winter of 1989/90. Originally the canal was puddled with
clay.

In 1826 the embankment collapsed and a mass of rubble dammed
the river below. Water and rubble filled up and totally destroyed
the lower pits of Chirk Bank Colliery. Amazingly no men were
down the pit for the first time in several years. Despite local
history books that state the contrary, I am reliably informed
that new pits were dug further up the bank in 1829 and that
the colliery worked until the 1840's. Another breach of the canal
occurred in 1903.

The houses below the towpath were built in the late 19th century and,
like many in the area, are built of Ruabon brick with Welsh slate roofs.
Slate was exported by canal as far as London from a quarry near
Llangollen.

[47] The Ceiriog Viaduct, designed by Travers, Morgan and Partners, consists of a 470 metre long 'constant depth cellular pre-stressed concrete box girder' which was cast in 32 segments on the south bank to form a continuous section which was then launched across the 8 piers (and temporary steel piers) in the valley at a rate of 15 metres a week during 1990. It is the longest concrete bridge of its type in Britain and stands 30 metres above the Afon Ceiriog.

Let us hope that it is stronger than the engineer's bridge built for site access which, much to the amusement of a local man who had told them that it was too low, gave way during the winter floods of 1989/90.

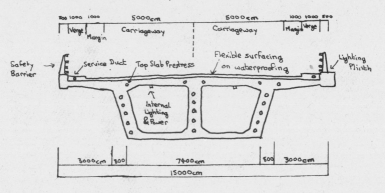

A TYPICAL CROSS SECTION OF THE CEIRIOG VIADUCT

   Courtesy of Travers, Morgan and Partners

[48] Llangollen Canal, first known as the Ellesmere Canal, was planned in 1791 to link the rivers Mersey, Severn and Dee. Due to financial problems and competition from another canal to Shrewsbury this was never completed.

The canal through Chirk opened in 1802. William Jessop was the Chief Engineer while Thomas Telford was the General Agent, Surveyor, Engineer, Architect and Overlooker of the Works, all of which he completed to such a fine standard that he eventually replaced Jessop.

The aqueduct was started on 17th June 1796. Work on the 21 metre
high structure was completed 5 years later. Cast-iron plates
were set in the bottom of the masonry channel to hold the
water. An iron trough appears to have been added later,
perhaps after the success of the iron Pontcysyllte Aqueduct
over the River Dee, but surprisingly no records have been
found relating to this major refit.

1840 ENGRAVING OF CHIRK AQUEDUCT

In 1805, the waterway was linked with the Chester Canal via
Ellesmere and this, in turn, joined with the Wirral section of
the Ellesmere Canal leading to the Mersey. In 1808 the
arm to Llangollen was completed and 5 years later the
Ellesmere and Chester Canal Companies, now dependent on
each other, became one.

A later amalgamation was made with the Birmingham and
Liverpool Junction Canal Company whilst in 1846 several other
interests joined to form the Shropshire Union Railways and Canal

Company. The SURCC was leased to the London and North Western Railway who kept the canal open into the 20th century to compete with their rival, Great Western Railway. Other companies increased canal tolls to boost dependence on train services that they had invested in, or used the filled in canals to lay the railway tracks.

In 1923 the LNWR became part of the London, Midland and Scottish Railway Company and was later nationalised. Since 1963 it has been run by the state-owned British Waterways Board. Maintenance costs are, in part, paid by licensing the many pleasure craft that now travel the canal systems and, to a lesser degree, by the thousands of coarse fishermen who hook out roach and perch, only to reinstate them, in a worse condition, to their watery home at the end of the day.

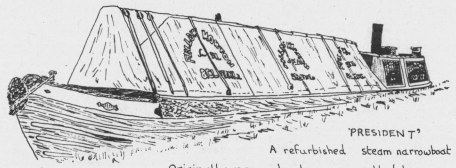

'PRESIDENT'
A refurbished steam narrowboat

Originally narrowboats were pulled by horses but as early as 1860 a steam engine was fitted to the Grand Junction Canal Company's narrowboat 'Pioneer.' By the end of 1860 at least ten steam powered narrowboats were being constructed.

[49] Chirk Tunnel, completed in 1802, was mined through solid rock. The 420 metre length has a handrail all the way. Beware, keep your dogs leashed — a friend did not and in the dark his dog just walked off the towpath into the water. The rescue that ensued gave the owner a few scratches.

westwards CHIRK BANK to PONT FAEN

From the towpath turn left onto the road and go over the bridge [50] and then take the kissing-gate on your right in about 100 metres. Curve right noting the hollow-way, probably the old Norman road, ahead. Beside it is the former site of the Glyn Valley Tramway road-bridge. Cross the track and follow the woodland boundary in view of a yellow-brick house [51].

Cross the railway [52] and, in the second field, take the stile on your right. Descend the track (the original course of the Glyn Valley Tramway). Turn first right and right again, opposite a dovecote [53] in a barn roof, to reach Pont Faen. Do not cross the bridge unless you want another view of Chirk Viaduct and Aqueduct, or you wish to turn right and first left up the path to Chirk Castle Gates [54].

eastwards PONT FAEN to CHIRK BANK

Do not cross the bridge unless you want a view of Chirk Viaduct and Aqueduct, or you wish to turn right and first left up the path to Chirk Castle Gates [54]. A route across the aqueduct is given later.

Fork right and then first left after looking up to your right to see a dovecote [53] in a barn roof. Beyond the cottage, ignore a gated track then take the next track on your left, again the former course of the Glyn Valley Tramway.

Turn left when you reach the field. The path follows the woodland boundary, crosses the railway [52] and goes through another field in view of a yellow-brick house [51]. Cross the track and follow the sunken path to the kissing-gate.

Turn left along the road to the canal bridge [50] beside Chirk Bank Post Office.

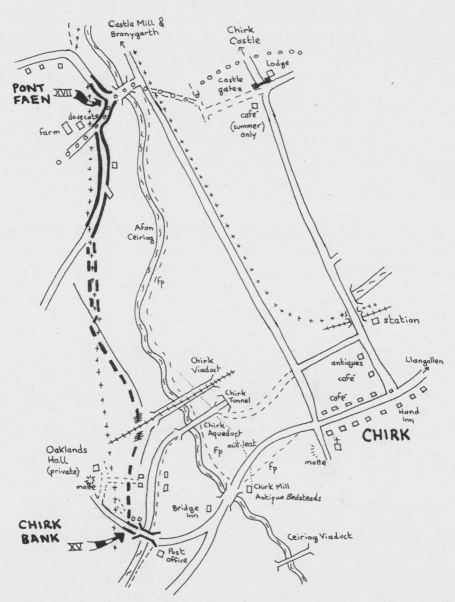

points of interest

[50] The road here was originally part of the London-Holyhead route. Then, in 1810, Telford built the lower road (at the foot of the hill) with an easier gradient. After completion, in 1825, no gradient on the route exceeded 1 in 22.

In 1810 the white house above the canal bridge was the Canal Tavern but in order to pick up the passing trade the landlord moved down to the Bridge Inn at the junction of the two roads.

[51] The yellow-brick house is Oaklands Hall, built in the latter half of the 19th century for a Mr Parry Jones. The east wing, a castellated folly, has an inscription which states that it was built in October 1877 by Amelia Louise Parry Jones in memory of a friend who died in Venice.

The building on the opposite side of the field was a coachhouse and has now been converted to a private residence. The estate once had its own private footbridge over the canal; the remains of this can be seen from the canal towpath below.

OAKLANDS HALL : NOW A PRIVATE RETIREMENT HOME

In the garden of the Hall is the mound of a Norman motte and bailey, and on the other side of the valley, below St Mary's Church at Chirk, is another.

A motte and bailey was a wooden tower built on a mound and surrounded by a courtyard and wooden fortifications. William the Conqueror's armies raised these castles all over England, with a great number on the Welsh border, using the labour of the conquered Anglo-Saxons.

BUILDING THE FIRST BRITISH MOTTE AT HASTINGS
Detail from the Bayeux Tapestry

The Pipe Rolls of 1213 recorded a payment of £5 for a bretasche (part of the wooden fortification) on the Chirk motte which may have been 'Peveral's Tower' on the 'waters of the Ceiriog', recorded in the reign of Henry I (1100-1135). In 1086 it is recorded that 'Peveril' held the Lordship of Ellesmere from Duke Roger, whilst in 1155 William Peverill was convicted of sorcery and of having poisoned Earl Ranalf of Chester by using witchcraft.

The sunken path by the kissing-gate may be the Norman road to the Oaklands Hall motte.

[52] Chirk Viaduct was built by Henry Robertson for the Chester-Shrewsbury Railway and was finished in 1848. It became part of the Great Western Railway and now forms part of the British Rail network. The viaduct towers 30 metres above the river and 9 metres above the river and 9 metres above the earlier canal aqueduct.

[53] Dovecotes, often separate purpose-built structures, were kept to supply fresh eggs and meat. This form of food production was brought to Britain by the Normans but has declined this century, partly because of advances in food storage and arable agricultural methods and partly because local crops would suffer with so many birds nearby.

18TH CENTURY DOVECOTE AT PONT FAEN FARM

Over 15 dovecotes can still be found in Wrexham Maelor whilst at least 50 still exist in Clwyd. Two more are mentioned in this guide.

[54] Chirk Castle Gates were fabricated by the Davies brothers of Croesfoel, near Wrexham, an outlier of the Myddleton Estate. Originally commissioned in 1712, by 1720 they had been erected at the north court of the castle for Sir Richard Myddleton, the third baronet and Lord Lieutenant of Denbighshire. In 1770 they were moved to the New Hall entrance then, when the railway was built, moved again to the foot of the driveway leading to the station.

The condition attached to the sale of land for the railway was that a station be built and that all passenger trains stop there. This condition has never been rescinded.

Note the 'bloody hand' above the gates. In legend the hand symbol arises from a race to settle an inheritance dispute of the Myddleton family. A supporter of the loser cut off the winner's hand as he finished the race.

Another legend states that the hand is a curse upon the Myddleton family which can only be removed if a prisoner survives 10 years in Chirk Castle dungeon. A daunting prospect!

Chirk, Rhuddan, Ruthin and Dinas Brân castles have all been owned by the family.

Above: DETAIL FROM THE CASTLE GATE

Below: CHIRK CASTLE GATES

westwards PONT FAEN to BRONYGARTH

Before Pont Faen [55] take the lane on your left and at the first bend cross the stile and descend the track. On your right you can again see the original course of the Glyn Valley Tramway. Follow the River Ceiriog [56] through meadows and woodland [57] with a view over trout ponds [58].

Beyond the woodland, follow the clear green causeway veering left to join an enclosed track and pass a huge black poplar tree. At the top of the lane, past Well Cottage [59], turn right at the T-junction to pass The Stables and The Old School [60]. The road appears to head straight for Chirk Castle [61]. In 600 metres, beyond four limekilns [62] built into the hillside, turn right to reach Castle Mill Bridge, and the end of the Maelor Way. Offa's Dyke Path and the Extension to Pontcysyllte can be followed from here. For the station cross the bridge and turn right then first left.

eastwards BRONYGARTH to PONT FAEN

Across the bridge on the Welsh (north) side of the River Ceiriog [56] is a summer path to Chirk Castle [61]. From the English (south) bank head uphill and turn left at the T-junction. After only a hundred metres you pass four limekilns [62] built into the hillside. Just beyond The Old School [60] and Smithy Cottage, descend the lane to your left, passing Well Cottage [59]. Cross the next track and go through gates by The Hollow. At the end of the lane, after an enormous black poplar tree, follow the green causeway half-right. The Way continues through cleared woodland [57] above the Ceiriog with a view over trout ponds [58].

Follow the riverside path through meadows to the lane. On your left is part of the original course of the Glyn Valley Tramway [45]. At the bottom of the lane you reach Pont Faen [55].

NOT TO SCALE

Some areas have been expanded
to show directions in detail.

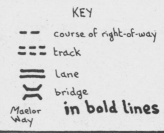

KEY

- - - course of right-of-way

☐ ☐ ☐ track

= = = lane

X bridge

in bold lines

Maelor Way

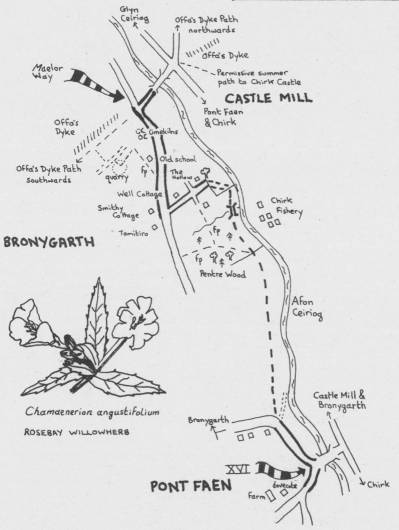

Glyn
Ceiriog

Offa's Dyke Path
northwards

Offa's Dyke

Permissive summer
path to Chirk Castle

CASTLE MILL

Maelor
Way

Pont Faen
& Chirk

Offa's
Dyke

limekilns

Old school

Offa's Dyke Path
southwards

quarry

fp

The
Hollow

Well Cottage

BRONYGARTH

Smithy
Cottage

Chirk
Fishery

Tamikiro

fp

Pentre Wood

fp

Afon
Ceiriog

Chamaenerion angustifolium
ROSEBAY WILLOWHERB

Bronygarth

Castle Mill &
Bronygarth

XVI

PONT FAEN

farm

dovecote

Chirk

97

points of interest

[55] In the seventeenth century, John Ogilby, as 'cosmographer' to the king, published a book of road maps. The main road from Chester to Cardiff crossed Pont Faen. At that time the road to Llangollen was shown on the south side of the river (the Maelor Way follows its course westwards) as it was only in the late 19th century that the turnpike or toll road on the north side of the river was built, alongside the route of the Glyn Valley Tramway.

The Cardiff road headed through Weston Rhyn to Selattyn while the Chester road ascended, what is now only a footpath, to the next junction. The next part of the road has been swallowed up and partly destroyed by the Chirk Castle Estate, although I can find no record of its legal diversion. When the castle is open it can be seen as a hollow-way crossing the first bend of the entrance drive and also crossing the permissive path from Ty'n-y-cil. The road shown to 'Oswastree' (Oswestry) ran through the riverside meadow and was closed in the Quarter Sessions of July 1863.

[56] Before the Ice Ages, the rivers now known as the Dee and Ceiriog curved south beyond Chirk and led into what is now the River Severn. Chirk is built on glacial drifts.

[57] The woodland path was cleared and steps were built by a Manpower Services team. The local farmer remembers a flight of stone steps, parallel to these but further from the river. Miners would use these on the way to Black Park Colliery at Chirk. Clearance of the path provided a habitat for foxglove, rosebay willowherb and yellow pimpernel.

YELLOW PIMPERNEL
Lysimachia nemorum

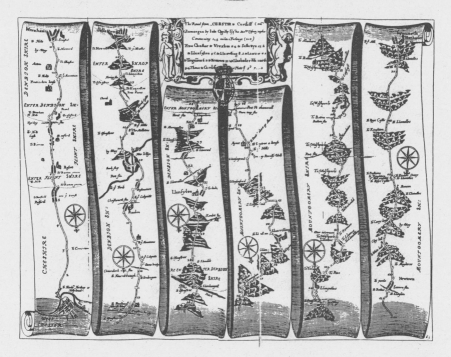

Above: MAP DEPICTING
THE ROAD FROM
CHESTER TO CARDIFF
IN 1675.

Beside: A SECTION OF
THE CHESTER TO
CARDIFF ROAD ACROSS
PONT VAINE (PONT FAEN)

SIR THOMAS 'MIDLETONS'
WAS POSSIBLY THE
ORIGINAL HOUSE NAMED
'CREAUGWYNION'
(now demolished but above
the present house of that name.)

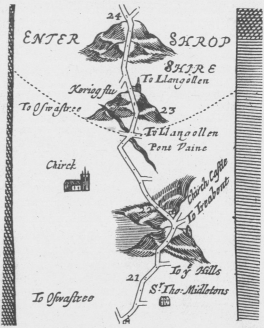

[58] A former mill race now feeds the trout breeding ponds where strong security measures deter poachers. At feeding time the noise of jumping fish carries to this side of the river Recent reports have shown that factory farming of this type may pollute water supplies both with excreta and chemicals.

[59] Well Cottage was once two cottages, homes for workers at the Bronygarth limekilns. The name Bronygarth translates as breast of the ridge; like many Welsh place names, it refers to topographical features.

[60] The Old School log books date from 1895 when the school opened with 18 girls and 9 boys. By the 1900's the attendance had risen to over a hundred although records of absenteeism show that the school's pupils enjoyed 'Public Teas' at the Castle Mill Mission Rooms; blackberry picking in September; and acorn picking, presumably to feed their pigs, in October. There were also several instances of truancy due to 'bush beating' for the Chirk Castle Estate's hunting during January.

[61] Chirk Castle has been continuously inhabited since it was built for Sir Roger Mortimer in the reign of Edward I. The lordship of Chirkland was created in 1282 for Mortimer who, like Edward, was a grandson of King John. Edward had just successfully invaded Wales and created several new lordships for his army's commanders in order to retain possession of the country. Mortimer's ambitions first led to power as the Justiciar of all Wales in 1308 and later to his downfall in 1322. He ended his life in the Tower of London after 4 years imprisonment.

The castle was bought, in 1595, by Sir Thomas Myddleton, a native of Denbigh and the Lord Mayor of London. The Myddleton family still live here although the property is now managed by the National Trust.

Extensive literature on the castle, its interior decoration, art treasures and history, can be obtained from the castle or found in public libraries. The attractive gardens support a variety of ornamental trees and plants.

19TH CENTURY ENGRAVING OF CHIRK CASTLE

CASTLE OPENING TIMES (MAY CHANGE SLIGHTLY YEAR TO YEAR)
Easter - Sept 30th 12-5pm excl. Mons & Sats, open Bank Hol. Mons.
1st October - last Sun. in October 12-5pm Sats & Suns only.

[62] These limekilns were once served by a short tramway which ran across Castle Mill Bridge to join the Glyn Valley Tramway. On the roadside are the unloading bays, the main furnaces behind these would have been filled from the top.

Crushed limestone was kilned here at a temperature of over 900°c. After the carbon dioxide had been released in the process, the remaining alkaline powder — known as slaked, hydrated or burnt lime or just 'lime' — was used for binding mortar and as a whitewash. It was also, and is still, used as an acidity stabiliser for 'manure-sick' and other acid soils, and in industry as a flux for steel.

around the mere – A CIRCULAR WALK FROM HANMER

3 miles / 5 kilometres

INTRODUCTION

The western shore of the mere is the private property of the Gredington Estate but footpaths can be followed along the eastern side and in a wide circle around the estate returning to Hanmer on a country lane. The mere supports a variety of wildfowl including Canada goose, tufted duck and great crested grebe. House martins swoop low over the water on summer evenings searching for flies. There are also some interesting wildflowers such as gipsywort - a nettle look-a-like that once had its dark staining juice used by fortune tellers to give them a swarthy gipsy look.

Lycopus europaeus

GIPSYWORT

WALK DIRECTIONS

Take the kissing-gate onto the mere shore. Follow the path across 3 stiles, then turn half-left to a gate at the top of the field. Turn right and follow the track to its end. Turn left beside the house and use the small gate on the right to follow the woodland boundary. After two fields cross the stile into the wood, leaving it immediately by the next stile on your right. The old road inside the wood is said to be the ancient salt road from the Wich Valley heading south across Breadenheath. After another two fields take the stile at the corner of the wood, beside a horse-jump, and then, beyond the next stile, ascend the narrow field and go through the gate.

Cross the field until you reach the bridgegate ahead. Do not use this but turn right and in 300 metres go through a gateway at the far end of the field. In another 15 metres or so, beyond

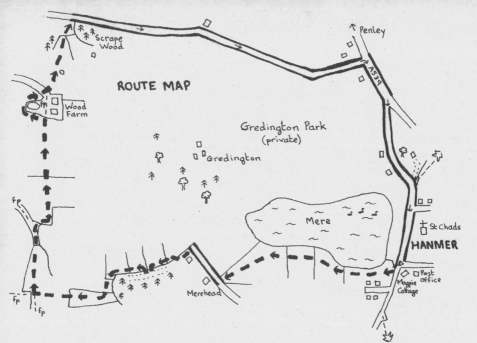

ROUTE MAP

Scrape Wood

Penley

A539

Wood Farm

Gredington Park (private)

Gredington

fp

Mere

St Chads

HANMER

fp

Merehead

Post Office

Magpie Cottage

fp

another gateway, turn right and cross the almost hidden stile in the corner. Follow the field boundary to your right and, at the protruding field corner, continue ahead crossing a stile as you aim for farm buildings. Keep the farm and pond to your right to cross the drive then continue to the distant corner of the next field. Drop down to the stile and go ahead to a stile below the lane. Turn right. In a kilometre, at the T-junction turn right and right again to Hanmer.

Branta canadensis

CANADA GOOSE

return beside the llangollen canal

The return journey is easy to follow. However, there is one section where the towpath has completely eroded and the alternative route, which includes Colemere Country Park, is given below. Beware, although the map and the directions use bridge numbers (given in brackets), the metal number plates on each bridge regularly go missing so you may wish to check the features of local topography that are given on the map as you proceed [Letters refer to points of interest.]

westwards GRINDLEY BROOK via ELLESMERE to GLEDRID BRIDGE

Ascend beside the locks from the canal bridge (28) at the east of the A41. After a mile note the filled-in Whitchurch Arm [A] by the New Mills lifting bridge (31). In another 4 miles, after Platt Lane Bridge (43) you may find it easier to walk along one of the tracks either side of the canal to avoid overgrowth. The short Prees Branch [B] forks to the right beyond Roving Bridge (46).

After passing through Whixall Moss [C] you leave the canal at Hampton Bank Bridge (50). Turn Left and cross the bridge. Take the first right turn: this takes you to the village of Lyneal. Turn right before the timber-framed cottage. Continue ahead by the thatched cottage then turn left opposite the school. From the car park at Cole Mere [D] take the path either way around the mere to the lane at the far side. Turn right to pass the thatched Little Mill Cottage, then left onto the canal towpath. Blake Mere is passed on your right before you go through the Ellesmere Tunnel (57). In less than a mile,

Llangollen Canal

	Route
⟩⟨	Bridge
⟩⟨⟨	Lift Bridge
⌄	Lock

27 — Dismantled Rly.
28 — GRINDLEY BROOK
29 — A41
30 —
31 — New Mills, Whitchurch Arm
32 — A525 Wrexham Road
33 —
34 —
35 —
37 —
38 —
39 —
40 —
41 —
42 —
43 — PH, Platt Lane
44 —
45 —
46 — Roving Bridge, Prees Branch, Whixall Moss
47 —
48 — Bettisfield Bridge Shop
49 —
50 — Hampton Bank Br.
51 —
52 — LYNEAL

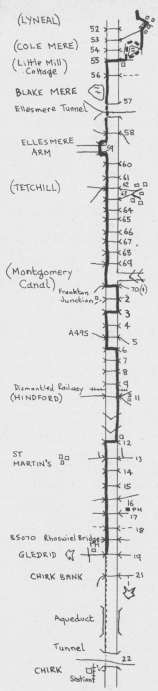

(LYNEAL)
(COLE MERE)
(Little Mill Cottage)
BLAKE MERE
Ellesmere Tunnel
ELLESMERE ARM
(TETCHILL)
(Montgomery Canal)
Frankton Junction
A495
Dismantled Railway (HINDFORD)
ST MARTIN'S
BS070 Rhoswiel Bridge
GLEDRID
CHIRK BANK
Aqueduct
Tunnel
CHIRK Station

52
53
54
55
56
57
58
59
60
61
62
63
64
65
66
67
68
69
70(?)
2
3
4
5
6
7
8
9
11
12
13
14
15
16
PH
17
18
19
21
22

a short arm heads under White Bridge (59) to the town of Ellesmere **[E]** well worth visiting, both for its interesting buildings and shops as well as The Mere on the other side of town which supports a wide range of wildfowl and boasts a heronry.

Continue along the main canal passing Frankton Junction **[F]** where the Montgomery Canal **[G]** forks to your left beyond Peter's Bridge (69) in about 4 miles/6km. Another 6 miles/10km through St Martin's Moor brings you to Gledrid Bridge (19) where you join the Maelor Way (see Section XV)

eastwards GLEDRID BRIDGE via ELLESMERE to GRINDLEY BROOK

From Gledrid Bridge (19) (see section XV) the towpath is clear for 6 miles/10km to Frankton Junction **[F]** (between bridges 70 and 69) where the Montgomery Canal **[G]** forks to the right. After another 4 miles/6km, a short arm heads under White Bridge (59) to the town of Ellesmere **[E]** both for its interesting buildings and shops as well as The Mere on the other side of town which supports a wide range of wildfowl and boasts a heronry.

As you follow the main canal you go under a short tunnel (57) and pass Blake Mere on your left. From Little Mill Bridge (55) beside the thatched mill cottage, cross the bridge and, beyond the cottage, take the path either way around Cole Mere **[D]** to the car park. Turn left along the lane. At the T-junction opposite the school in the village of Lyneal, turn right. Ignore the next left turn just beyond a thatched cottage. At the T-junction turn left and, at the main road, turn left to rejoin the canal at Hampton Bank Bridge (50).

After passing through Whixall Moss [C], the short Prees Branch [B], forks to your right before Roving Bridge (47). Beyond Roundthorn Bridge (44) the towpath is often overgrown and it is easier to follow the track alongside to Platt Lane Bridge (43). In another 4 miles/6km note the filled-in Whitchurch Arm [A] by the New Mills lifting bridge (31). Leave the canal beyond the bottom lock at Grindley Brook. Join the South Cheshire Way or the Sandstone Trail at this bridge (28) or turn left to the A41, the Shropshire Way or the Maelor Way.

THE ELLESMERE TUNNEL

Mimulas guttatus

MONKEYFLOWER

This yellow flower which can be
found growing in profusion
along the canal during summer
is a native of Unalaska Island in
North America and was first
introduced to Britain in 1812.

Tanacetum vulgare
TANSY

Another yellow-flowered
plant, its leaves were
once popular for flavour-
ing apple pies.

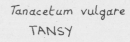

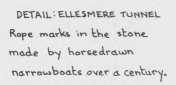

DETAIL: ELLESMERE TUNNEL
Rope marks in the stone
made by horsedrawn
narrowboats over a century.

points of interest

[A] When the Ellesmere Branch had been cut as far as the junction with the Chester Canal in 1805, Whitchurch had been bypassed. However, there was an obvious need for a trading link with the town and in 1811 a new arm was opened into the town centre. This was closed in 1944 after nationalisation but the old towpath remains as the most direct route for walkers wishing to visit the town, less than two kilometres distant.

[B] Only the first three miles or so of the Prees Branch were ever completed and, like the Whitchurch Arm, it was closed in 1944. In 1974 a mile was reopened to serve the Black Prince Marina. The canal branch is an SSSI (Site of Special Scientific Interest).

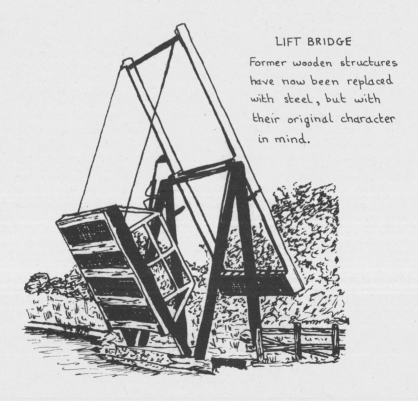

LIFT BRIDGE
Former wooden structures have now been replaced with steel, but with their original character in mind.

[c] Whixall and Fenns Mosses are protected as SSSIs although there is still a right to cut peat here both for local people and for a commercial concern. Croxden Horticultural Limited caused an outcry during 1990 as they increased cutting from 15,000 tonnes to 60,000 tonnes thus draining large areas of the moss and disturbing wildlife. In the past the slow rate of peat cutting let sphagnum moss recolonise old cuts.

This raised peat moor is the third largest in Britain and is dominated by purple moor-grass and cross-leaved heath. It supports sundew, an interesting plant that catches and digests insects. A great variety of insect life has been recorded here, including 11 endangered species and 16 of the 42 known British dragonflies, one of which, the white-faced darter, is normally restricted to Scotland.

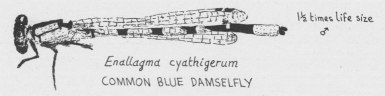

1½ times life size
♂

Enallagma cyathigerum
COMMON BLUE DAMSELFLY

Dragonflies (the term includes damselflies) lay their eggs in peat or mud near water. The larvae that emerge may live for up to two years in the water before entering the air where they metamorphose into the adult or imago state to breed. Perhaps the most abundant dragonfly is the common blue damselfly which can be seen in large numbers along the canal during summer. The male is blue with black markings while the female is often brown or dull green. Despite common folklore, dragonflies do not sting although if picked up they mimic the body motion of a stinging insect.

MATING
Common blue damselflies

The canal beside Whixall Moss also supports a large number of butterflies. Wall brown, speckled wood and small copper are common here.

Lycaena phlaeas
SMALL COPPER

[D] Researchers differ as to the derivation of the name Cole in Colebrook and Cole Mere. It may be derived from collis (hill), coll (hazelwood), cole (charcoal) or even a Saxon personal name.

CANADA GEESE AT COLE MERE

[E] The tourist trade at Ellesmere is aimed at boaters on their way to Llangollen, and weekend visitors who come to see the meres. Consequently the town is well kept with more than the average number of antique shops. Beside the canal basin stand the warehouses, dating from Telford's day and signwritten with the later name of the canal company: Shropshire Union Railways and Canal Company.

As long ago as the 8th century there was a church in the town. After the Norman invasion the 1068 Domesday Book records the name of the town as 'Ellesmelles' and states: 'Earl Edwin held it (before 1066). 4½ hides (about 180 hectares). In lordship 5 ploughs; 10 ploughmen, 36 villagers and 14 smallholders with 2 priests have 14 ploughs. A mill. Before (1066) paid £10; now £20'. Women and children were not included so we could guess at a population of about 250. This thriving area had just had its tax doubled!

In the late 18th century the canal brought renown to Ellesmere whilst a trade directory of 1828 stated that the principal trades here were tanning and malting. In the latter part of the 19th century the Woodard Corporation founded Ellesmere College, a private school which stands grandly on the hill to the south of the canal.

[F] The Ellesmere Canal (now the Llangollen Canal) main line was originally intended to be cut southwards from Frankton Junction and then southeast to Shrewsbury, with a branch from Frankton to the Montgomery Canal. This branch was started in 1794 and completed fairly quickly but the main line was only cut to Weston Lullingfields. What had been intended as a branch to Ellesmere now became the main line and was continued to the Chester Canal and completed in 1805 while the Weston Lullingfields' route became only a branch. After the decline of the canal system the locks at Frankton fell into disrepair and were only renovated in 1987.

[G] The Montgomery Canal from Frankton Junction to Newtown is 38 miles long. The short northern section through the

ELLESMERE CANAL BASIN

first four locks was the intended main line to the River Severn and was cut by 1796. The next section was known as the Llanymynech Branch and opened a year later. The final section, the original Montgomery Canal, to Newtown opened in 1819.

In 1936 a breach in the canal wall stopped navigation and in 1944 the canal was closed. Restoration started in 1967 resulting in a seven mile section near Welshpool being opened by the Prince of Wales in 1974.

Details of current work (volunteers are always needed) are available from the British Waterways Board (see the display board at Frankton Junction) or the Shropshire Union Canal Society, Working Party Organiser: Jeffrey Munro, 198 Oldbury Road, Rowley Regis, Worley, West Midlands B65 0NW. Telephone 021 561 5747.

The full length of the Montgomery Canal towpath is open to walkers. Three Ordnance Survey Landrangers cover the route: 126, 136 and 137.

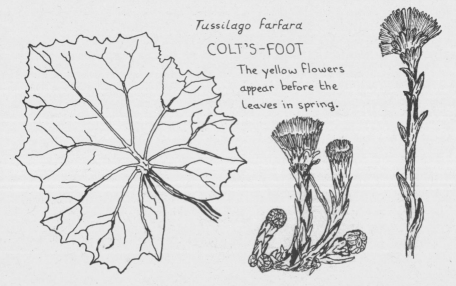

Tussilago farfara

COLT'S-FOOT

The yellow flowers appear before the leaves in spring.

extension to pontcysyllte

BRONYGARTH to PONTCYSYLLTE AQUEDUCT returning along
the Llangollen Canal to CHIRK BANK

From the western end of the Maelor Way, cross the bridge over
the River Ceiriog, pass St Catherine's Chapel and follow the
sign 'Llwybr Clawdd Offa' (offa's Dyke Path) up the lane opposite.
Fork right where a lane goes downhill. At the bend beyond
the half-timbered building, Crogen Wladlys, cross the stile
and ascend to the shallow pass and another stile. To your
right, as you continue, is Chirk Castle. Ahead is Lindisfarne
College in the distance. Beyond another stile you reach
Ty'n-y-groes (house of the cross) where you turn right and
immediately left. The cross referred to is possibly that formed
by a Roman road, an extension of Stryt-y-veri, that may go
under the house at this point. A *summer only permissive path*
leads to the castle from this junction.

LINDISFARNE COLLEGE formerly WYNNSTAY HALL

Pass the dovecote in a barn roof on your left and at the
next bend take the stile on your left and veer half-right
over two fields. Turn right and immediately left along the
Lane. Fork right at the next junction and go over the
crossroad. In about a kilometre take the stile on your

113

right and drop down over fields to cross the A5. Take
the track almost opposite, beside a house built to a
Canadian design: the rooms are on the first floor to
stay above snowdrifts!

Over the brow of the hill, a stile on your right takes
you along the bank to the road again. Cross 'Irish
Bridge'. The bridge was named after the Irish 'navvies'
(builders of navigations) who laboured and toiled, away
from their native land and without JCB's or Guinness,
to cut this long narrow ditch for English narrowboats.

To reach Pontcysyllte Aqueduct go ahead along the
towpath. On the way look for a nature trail on your
right which winds its way through the woodland of
Tan-y-cut, managed by Wrexham Maelor Borough Council.
The name of the wood is an unusual mixture of Welsh
(tan-y = below the) and English slang (cut=a canal).

By following the canal in the opposite direction you can
reach Chirk Station (3km) or the Maelor Way at Chirk Bank
(4km).

PONTCYSYLLTE AQUEDUCT

route map EXTENSION TO PONTCYSYLLTE

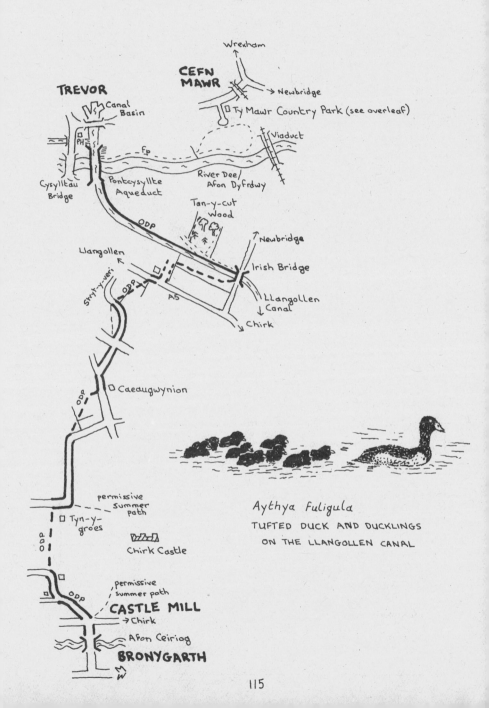

Wrexham

CEFN MAWR

TREVOR

→ Newbridge

Canal Basin

Ty Mawr Country Park (see overleaf)

PH

Viaduct

Fp

River Dee/
Afon Dyfrdwy

Cysylltau Bridge

Pontcysyllte Aqueduct

Tan-y-cut Wood

ODP

Newbridge

Llangollen

Irish Bridge

Stryt-y-veri

ODP

A5

Llangollen Canal

Chirk

ODP

Caeaugwynion

Aythya Fuligula

TUFTED DUCK AND DUCKLINGS

ON THE LLANGOLLEN CANAL

permissive summer path

ODP

Tyn-y-groes

Chirk Castle

permissive summer path

ODP

CASTLE MILL

→ Chirk

Afon Ceiriog

BRONYGARTH

115

TY MAWR

COUNTRY

PARK

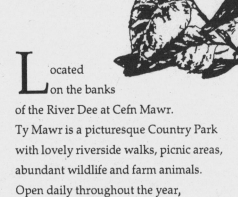

L ocated
on the banks
of the River Dee at Cefn Mawr.
Ty Mawr is a picturesque Country Park
with lovely riverside walks, picnic areas,
abundant wildlife and farm animals.
Open daily throughout the year,
Ty Mawr has something to offer all ages.

For further information telephone:
The Park Rangers : Ruabon (0978) 822780
The Tourist Development Officer : Wrexham (0978) 290444 Ext. 2165

Ty Mawr Country Park,
Cae Gwilym Road,
Cefn Mawr, Wrexham, Clwyd.

THE
WELSH
Borderlands
WREXHAM
MAELOR

offa's dyke path

This 177 mile/285 kilometre National Trail, waymarked with an acorn symbol, runs from Chepstow beside the River Severn, to Prestatyn on the North Wales coast. Apart from the Pennine Way it is probably the best known trail in Britain and follows Offa's Dyke, south of the River Dee. North of the river it heads to the west of Rudbon Mountain and over the Clwydian Range to the coast. As one might expect for such a long trail, the scenery is varied and the route has many points of interest.

The 8th century earthwork - Offa's Dyke - that the trail mainly follows was built, possibly in just a few weeks, by King Offa of Mercia. It was probably a defensive measure, similar to Saxon town ditches.

COIN

GUIDES

Offa's Dyke Path North: Knighton to Prestatyn by Ernie and Kathy Kay and Mark Richards ISBN 1 85410 016 5 £7·95 covers the northern part adequately with corrected Ordnance Survey Map sections. Although the guide only has directions one way, it is easy for anyone who can map-read to follow it the other. The guide also gives short extensions and circular walks to places of interest. The book has a showerproof cover and good photographs which may account for its high price. The main reason for buying it must surely be the map sections, as the instructions are difficult for those who cannot map-read and some junctions are poorly described or even missed.

Offa's Dyke Path South, authors as above. ISBN 1 85410 017 3 £7·95

Through Welsh Border Country following Offa's Dyke Path by Mark Richards. Thornhill Press. £4-50 is a 'Wainwright' style hand-written and illustrated guide which covers the whole length of the path starting from Prestatyn. There are no detailed walk directions but the hand-drawn section maps can be followed either way; surely the best guide and souvenir for the path so far.

Strip Maps for Offa's Dyke, Offa's Dyke Association £2-50. Nine strip maps cover the whole trail but the title might confuse someone looking for the dyke and not the path.

Route notes to accompany strip maps, South to North. ODA £1-00.
Route notes to accompany strip maps, North to South. ODA £1-00.
Where to stay ODA 75p   Try also the Ramblers' Association Yearbook.

The Offa's Dyke Association Book of Offa's Dyke Path by Frank Noble, ODA.   ISBN 0 9507227 0 7   This dated book is not a walking guide and the text is as wordy as the title. It contains a few general maps and some nice black and white photos

A guide to Offa's Dyke Path by Christopher Wright, Constable. ISBN 0 09 469140 1 £8-95. Good maps, and black and white photos characterise this slightly dated book that describes the path from south to north with only general directions.

Crwydro Clawdd Offa by Ifor Rees. Christopher Davies
ISBN 0 7154 0549 7 £1-50
Not a route guide but possibly the only Welsh book on the Path, it includes points of interest, poetry, and black and white photographs.

Offa's Dyke Path by Arthur Roberts MBE 45p Available from the Ramblers' Association, 1/5 Wandsworth Road, London.
Overall map, directions south-north, slightly outdated archaeological information.

south cheshire way

This trail marked with the ⌂ symbol, was planned partly by the Late Jack Baker. It meets the Maelor Way at Grindley Brook and links with the Mow Cop Trail at Ruston (which, in turn, links with the Gritstone Trail and the Staffordshire Way).

The inexpensive *Guide to the South Cheshire Way by Justin McCarthy, Mid-Cheshire Footpath Society* 75p has directions westwards. The guide, which suffers from the over-use of 44 different abbreviations and gives unnecessary footpath numbers, has rough strip maps and recommends the use of OS maps but does not give their references (Pathfinders SJ 44/54 64/74 65/75 85/95 Landrangers 117, 118, 119) The guide includes a food and accommodation list.

sandstone trail

Following the West Cheshire Ridge, formed from Triassic Sandstone, the walker has panoramic views over Cheshire and into Wales. The Trail, planned and executed by the Late Jack Baker, stretches 30 miles/48 kilometres between Frodsham and Grindley Brook and is waymarked throughout by the ⑤ symbol and managed by Cheshire Countryside Rangers.

The Sandstone Trail Walkers Guide by Cheshire County Council (90p) is a little out of date now, as minor changes have been made to the Trail, but a new guide is imminent.

shropshire way

This circular route of 125 miles / 201 kilometres can be joined by an 11 mile / 18 kilometre extension from Grindley Brook. The Shropshire Way also has a circular extension of 35 miles/58km that joins Offa's Dyke Path at Mainstone, near Clun. The route is waymarked with the silhouette of a buzzard in a white circle.

The Way passes through the hill country of South Shropshire where geological features, developed by nature and man, have created a landscape of outstanding beauty. The route crosses the River Severn over Abraham Darby's famous cast-iron bridge. The Severn Gorge here has become world famous as the birth-place of the Industrial Revolution.

There are many picturesque buildings on the Shropshire Way including the medieval castles of Clun, Stokesay, Ludlow, Shrewsbury and Moreton Cobbett, as well as the fine Tudor manor house at Wilderhope, now a Youth Hostel. The abbeys at Much Wenlock and Haughmond Hill are passed, together with many interesting village churches, some dating from Norman times.

The well-illustrated standard guidebook is *The Shropshire Way* by Robert Kirk, Thornhill Press   ISBN 0 946328 05 6   £2·75. This contains reasonably detailed sketch maps. The author recommends the use of 1:50 000 OS maps as well, although it would be difficult to get lost relying on the guide alone.

Ludford Bridge.

REPRODUCED FROM 'THE SHROPSHIRE WAY' BY KIND PERMISSION OF THE AUTHOR, ROBERT KIRK.

Further reading

The Buildings of Wales: Clwyd by Edward Hubbard, Penguin.

Canal to Llangollen by Thomas Pellow and Paul Bowen, Landscape Press.

Roman Britain from the Air by S.S. Frere & J.K. St Joseph, Cambridge University Press.

Overton Village Trail by Clwyd County Council.

The Glyn Valley Tramway by W.J. Milner, Oxford Publishing Company.

The Meres Trail Guide by Paul Byath, Ellesmere Branch of Shropshire Trust for Nature Conservation.

Davies Brothers, Gatesmiths by Ifor Edwards, Welsh Arts Council.

A complete guide to British Dragonflies by Andrew McGeeney, Jonathan Cape.

Domesday Book, Cheshire } edited by John Morris, Phillimore.
Domesday Book, Shropshire)

Llangollen Canal Cruising Guide edited by Robert Shopland, Waterways Productions.

The Buildings of England: Shropshire by Nikolaus Pevsner, Penguin.

RSPB Guide to Birdwatching in Clwyd.

The Ellesmere and Llangollen Canal by Edward Wilson, Phillimore & Co Ltd.

The Place Names of Cheshire (Part Four) by J McN Dodgson.

Rhyn Park Roman Fortress by G D B Jones, Border Counties Archaeology Group.

The Private Life of the Rabbit by R.M. Lockley, (Readers' Union).

Rabbits and their History by John Sheail, (Country Book Club).

Chapters from the History of Ellesmere by J.W. Nankivels, Lazarica Press.

Archaeologia Cambrensis   1874/76/77/79/80/88/99   1902/45/51

Overton in Days Gone By, by G S Howson, available at Clwyd County Reference Library.

History of the Maelor, typewritten manuscript by Derek Pratt at Clwyd County Reference Library.

Many documents and local history files for the area around the Maelor Way are available from:

County Library, Shire Hall, MOLD, Clwyd.

Wrexham Reference Library, WREXHAM, Clwyd.

Local Studies Library, Castle Gates, SHREWSBURY, Shropshire.

County Record Office, HAWARDEN, Clwyd.

County Record Office, RUTHIN, Clwyd.

County Record Office, Shire Hall, SHREWSBURY, Shropshire (appt. only).

Please note: the Record Offices need proof of identity.

complaints ABOUT PUBLIC FOOTPATHS

Footpaths, bridges, signposts, crops, ferocious dogs, bulls etcetera on public paths are dealt with by the councils listed below. I would be grateful for a copy of all letters sent or, if unsure which authority to write to, send two to me and I will pass one to the appropriate authority and another to the Ramblers' Association. Please send written complaints, do not telephone.

Footpaths within Wrexham Maelor (Maelor Way : Shellbrook to Wolvesacre):

Director of Public Works, Wrexham Maelor Borough Council, Rhostyllen, WREXHAM, Clwyd. LL14 4DU

Bridges and signposts within Clwyd including Wrexham Maelor:

Director of Highways and Transportation, Clwyd County Council, Shire Hall, MOLD, Clwyd CH7 6NF

Footpaths and bridges in Shropshire (Maelor Way: Shell Brook westwards):

Head of Countryside, Leisure Services Department, Shropshire CC, Winston Churchill Building, Radbrook Centre, Radbrook Road, SHREWSBURY, Shropshire SY3 9BJ

All problems in Cheshire (Maelor Way: Wolvesacre eastwards):

Country Heritage and Recreation Officer, Public Rights of Way Department, Cheshire County Council, Commerce House, Hunter Street, CHESTER CH1 2QP

ABOUT THIS GUIDE
Alterations, items of interest, comments etcetera to the author: Gordon Emery, 27 Gladstone Road, CHESTER, CH1 4BZ
If you require a reply please enclose a stamped addressed envelope.

walking groups in the area

Ramblers' Association, Wrexham Group.
Paul and Valerie Davies (Secretaries), 32 Peel Street, WREXHAM
Clwyd LL13 7TR   0978 362253

Ramblers' Association, Clwydian Group.
Val Blake (Secretary)   051 336 4970

Mid-Cheshire Footpath Society.
Bernard Wright, 64 Crossfields, Tarvin, Chester.   0829 40658

Whitchurch Walkers.
Mrs O.M. Bishop (Secretary), 10 Richmond Terrace, Whitchurch,
Shropshire.   0948 2322

Wrexham Rambling Club.
David Roberts (Secretary)   0978 359140

Rainbow Ramblers, Gwernymynydd, Mold.
Mary Garston (Secretary)   0352 740628

information ABOUT WREXHAM MAELOR
PLACES TO VISIT,   WHAT TO SEE AND WHERE TO STAY

For current information contact:

    Tourism Development Officer
    Wrexham Maelor Borough Council
    Guildhall
    WREXHAM
    Clwyd
    LL11 1AY

    0978 290444 Ext.2165

directory of services TO HELP YOU PLAN YOUR WALK

All the advertisers below (except the kennels) are directly on the Maelor Way or within easy walking distance. Most are marked on the section maps.

ABBREVIATIONS

B&B   Bed and Breakfast   WTB   Wales Tourist Board Member

♛ Tourist Board Crown Rating   R   Reservations only

ACCOMMODATION

Mill House   HIGHER WYCH   B&B   WTB ♛♛   Evening Meals (R)

     Beside the 14th century mill site

          0948 73362

Bryn Rossett Farm   HANMER   B&B   Pets Welcome   1 family, 1 double

                                  1 single

    Grade II listed building with exposed beams   WTB

         094 874 229

Hanmer Arms Village Hotel HANMER   B&B   WTB ♛♛♛♛

   Breakfast, Morning Coffee, Lunches, Afternoon Teas, Dinner

     Open to non-residents   094 874 532

Buck Farm   HANMER   B&B   WTB ♛♛ Commended   Dinner (R)

                                     for non-residents

    Vegetarian, Vegan and special diets catered for

          094 874 339

Bridge House PENLEY   B&B (R)   WTB ♛♛   Drying facilities

                                      Evening Meals (R)

   A spacious modernised farmhouse

          0978 73 763

ACCOMMODATION (continued)

Little Overton Farm OVERTON-ON-DEE   B&B   Double +Single
Rooms available
from £10 person.

     Farmhouse Bed and Breakfast

                 0978 73 592

Rhoswiel Lodge WESTON RHYN   B&B

A friendly house near the canal with well-kept gardens
                0691 777609

SHOPS

The Post Office HANMER
        General Store, Provisions, Post Office

D & M Evans OVERTON
        General Store, Provisions, Confectionery, Ice Cream

The Post Office OVERTON *wishes all walkers on the
Maelor Way a safe and happy journey*

CHIRK BANK Post Office
        General Store, Local Guides, Drinks, Ice Cream

PET BOARDING

Boarding Cattery, Tamitiro, Bronygarth, Oswestry. 0691 773003

*Boarding Kennels, Glenwyn, Garden Cottage, Plas Issa Lane
Penycae, Wrexham*   0978 820756

WALKS IN CLWYD »

EXPLORE THE VILLAGES, MOUNTAINS, WOODS AND WATERWAYS
OF CLWYD WITH THESE INFORMATIVE GUIDES.

EACH BOOKLET CONTAINS AN INTERESTING WALK — SHORTCUTS ARE
INCLUDED — WITH DIRECTIONS, A MAP AND LINE DRAWINGS OF
BUILDINGS, PLANTS AND ANIMALS.

26 DIFFERENT WALKING GUIDES AVAILABLE FROM BOOKSHOPS,
TOURIST INFORMATION OFFICES AND CLWYD LIBRARIES.
MOST STARTING POINTS ARE ON BUS ROUTES. 90p
EACH

Enquiries 0244 377955